ACTION RESEARCH FOR STUDENT TEACHERS

Sara Miller McCune founded SAGE Publishing in 1965 to support the dissemination of usable knowledge and educate a global community. SAGE publishes more than 1000 journals and over 800 new books each year, spanning a wide range of subject areas. Our growing selection of library products includes archives, data, case studies and video. SAGE remains majority owned by our founder and after her lifetime will become owned by a charitable trust that secures the company's continued independence.

Los Angeles | London | New Delhi | Singapore | Washington DC | Melbourne

SECOND EDITION

ACTION RESEARCH FOR STUDENT TEACHERS

COLIN FORSTER & RACHEL EPERJESI

Los Angeles | London | New Delhi
Singapore | Washington DC | Melbourne

Los Angeles | London | New Delhi
Singapore | Washington DC | Melbourne

SAGE Publications Ltd
1 Oliver's Yard
55 City Road
London EC1Y 1SP

SAGE Publications Inc.
2455 Teller Road
Thousand Oaks, California 91320

SAGE Publications India Pvt Ltd
B 1/I 1 Mohan Cooperative Industrial Area
Mathura Road
New Delhi 110 044

SAGE Publications Asia-Pacific Pte Ltd
3 Church Street
#10-04 Samsung Hub
Singapore 049483

Editor: James Clark
Senior assistant editor: Diana Alves
Production editor: Nicola Carrier
Copyeditor: Jane Fricker
Proofreader: Leigh C Smithson
Indexer: Colin Forster and Rachel Eperjesi
Marketing manager: Lorna Patkai
Cover design: Naomi Robinson
Typeset by: C&M Digitals (P) Ltd, Chennai, India
Printed in the UK

First edition published 2017, reprinted three times in 2018,
once 2019, 2020
This edition first published 2021

Library of Congress Control Number: 2020942331

British Library Cataloguing in Publication data

A catalogue record for this book is available from the
British Library

ISBN 978-1-5297-3033-3
ISBN 978-1-5297-3032-6 (pbk)

CONTENTS

Contents

ABOUT THE AUTHORS

Much to the surprise of anyone who meets him now, when he was a young man, **Colin Forster** spent two years working as an outdoor activities instructor and it was during this time that he developed an interest in education. He began his primary teaching career in southwest London before moving to Gloucestershire, where he continued to gain school leadership experience. He is currently a senior lecturer in primary education at the University of Gloucestershire, where he has gained considerable experience of primary teacher education course leadership and in supporting students, at both undergraduate and postgraduate level, with research projects focused on improving practice. His areas of interest include primary science, behaviour management and action research, and he has undertaken research into children's experience of homework in the primary years.

Rachel Eperjesi knew she wanted to be a teacher from the age of five. However, some rather poor careers advice led her to embark on a medical degree, which quickly resulted in her declaring it 'too messy' and she decided to follow her heart into teaching instead. After completing a BEd Hons, Rachel taught in Foundation Stage and Key Stage 1 (also quite messy) in Gloucestershire, as well as undertaking English consultancy for the local authority. She now works at the University of Gloucestershire, lecturing in primary English and professional studies, as well as currently leading the School Direct PGCE Primary course. Rachel has supported many students, both undergraduate and postgraduate, with research projects focusing on improving their educational practice.

ACKNOWLEDGEMENTS

This second edition was largely written during the period now known as 'The COVID-19 Lockdown'. This presented us with several challenges but we are very grateful for the ongoing encouragement and support that we received from so many people.

We would like to thank all of our students, from whom we learn so much every year, and in particular those who kindly gave their permission for us to use some extracts from their assignments in the text.

We are also grateful for the support and encouragement given by our colleagues at the University of Gloucestershire.

We would like to give enormous thanks to David Brookes for his excellent illustrations that enliven the book and kept us smiling throughout the writing process. Dave, you are marvellous!

We have had tremendous support from the team at SAGE, for which we are very grateful.

Finally, we would like to thank our respective families for their patience and support throughout.

NEW TO THIS EDITION

This second edition has been updated throughout with a new Critical Task feature introduced for reflection and evaluation with suggested responses, and new further reading for you to explore in relation to the chapter's content. New content has been added, including where action research fits in the world of education research, the skills and attributes needed by teachers undertaking action research, and how to write with clarity and purpose.

1

INTRODUCTION

OBJECTIVES FOR THIS CHAPTER

- To introduce the nature and purpose of action research as a methodology for professionals in a range of contexts to solve challenges related to their daily work
- To introduce the relevance of action research as a useful framework for new teachers to enhance and develop their practice through evidence-based evaluation
- To explore where action research fits in the world of education research
- To explore the skills and attributes needed by teachers undertaking action research
- To explain the structure of this book and how it might be used to support new and aspiring teachers undertaking an action research enquiry.

ACTION RESEARCH

Action research is a well-established methodology that enables practitioners in a range of professional contexts to solve problems and improve their practice (Koshy, 2010). It provides a framework within which professionals can identify problems or challenges in their work, ask themselves questions about 'how they are doing', and seek solutions or improvements through reviewing appropriate evidence; it is the systematic analysis of a range of relevant evidence that makes action research more than just everyday evaluation. As McNiff (2016b: 9) puts it:

- Action refers to what you do.
- Research refers to how you find out about what you do.

Action research is often characterised by a reflective and developmental cycle of activity, in which a practitioner identifies an aspect of their practice that they think they should develop and considers how they could find out how well they are currently doing with it. Next, they gather relevant evidence that provides some clues about the effectiveness of

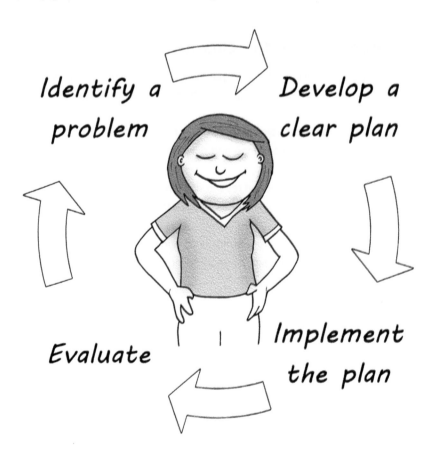

Identify a problem

Develop a clear plan

Implement the plan

Evaluate

this particular aspect of their work and, through reflecting on this evidence, the practitioner is able to identify some specific actions they might take to ensure that they have a more significant, positive impact on outcomes related to the particular issue they are focusing on. They then put these specific actions into practice and use evidence as the basis for making judgements about the impact of the developments, for further evaluation and identification of new steps for continued improvement . . . and so the cycles go on.

Action research is particularly relevant and commonly used within the teaching profession, and has particular applicability to those who are training to be teachers and those who are at an early stage in their teaching careers.

LEARNING TO TEACH

Learning to teach is not an easy process. There are many new ways of thinking, ways of talking and ways of doing that need to be learnt along the way. The specific phrasing of questions, the tone of voice, the speed of speech and the use of pauses, the correct vocabulary, the order in which information should be shared, the use of technology, the organisation of teaching resources, the role of children in the classroom, the ownership of children as learners, the use of feedback (verbal, written, child-centred) on learning, the use of body language, the quality and presentation of handwriting, the modelling of expectations, the response to children and young people in distress, the celebration of successes, the confident handling of anxious or aggressive parents, and the development of the secure subject knowledge required to teach (and this is not an exhaustive list by any means): all of these need to become embedded as part of the excellent teacher's daily practice. No wonder the old joke suggests that, with teaching, the first 40 years are the hardest.

The challenge for you, as a new or aspiring teacher, is that you will not be able to master all of these new aspects of excellent practice all at once and should focus on a small number of issues at a time, in order to embed them as part of your daily practice, all the while identifying new priorities for development and striving to master new skills.

Action research is all about improving teaching and learning with the aim of becoming an outstanding teacher. But we need to remember that, in the words of the song, 'It ain't what you do, it's the way that you do it' that gets results, so it is not about taking good practice 'off the shelf' and simply repeating what others have done.

ACTION RESEARCH AS EVIDENCE-BASED EVALUATION

Professor Dame Alison Peacock (quoted by the Chartered College of Teaching, n.d.) says this about the work of the Chartered College of Teaching, of which she is Chief Executive:

'We want to support the teaching profession to thrive in an optimal, research-informed way, providing the best possible education for children and young people'. It is clear that the purpose and processes of action research align well with this ambition. In this book, we suggest that, for new and aspiring teachers, action research is best thought of as 'evidence-based evaluation' and as a framework for new teachers to improve their practice. All good teachers evaluate their work, but it is the detailed analysis of evidence as the basis for evaluation that makes action research such a powerful process for improving practice and only through the effective use of evidence can an action-based project be claimed to be a kind of 'research'.

We have identified the stages in the cycles of action research in general terms, and here we identify how these stages look for new and aspiring teachers; we also outline how the stages of the process relate to the chapters in the rest of the book.

Stage one: Identify a 'problem' or an aspect of your practice that needs improving. This might relate to one of the issues identified earlier in this chapter and should be a substantive aspect of your practice which, if you can improve it, will have a significant impact on outcomes for the children or young people you are teaching. In Chapter 2, we will explore, in more detail, the kinds of issues that might be considered and the sources of evidence that would help a new or aspiring teacher identify their development priorities.

Stage two: Inform the development of your practice with knowledge. This is an often overlooked stage in the action research learning process, but it is important to be well informed about current thinking about good practice and to learn from research that has already been undertaken related to your particular focus. It is certainly better to do this reading before undertaking your project rather than afterwards. In Chapter 4, we will explore the benefits of engaging with appropriate literature and suggest some ways in which it can be done.

Stage three: Identify the things you would need to 'find out' in order to make secure judgements about the effectiveness of your teaching and, in particular, its impact on learning. We will explore this in detail in Chapter 3, in which we will consider how to define clear and appropriate objectives for your study.

Stage four: Identify the evidence that would enable you to find out what you need to know in order to improve your practice and develop a rigorous and ethical plan for gathering evidence. In Chapter 5, we will discuss the ethical considerations and practical actions that should be addressed when undertaking a school-based enquiry and, in Chapter 6, we will explore how a new or aspiring teacher might plan to gather useful and insightful evidence for their project.

Stage five: Gather relevant evidence about your practice and analyse it to gain real and meaningful insights into the impact your teaching is having on the learning of children or young people. We will discuss, in Chapter 8, how you can 'capture' appropriate evidence, taking account of the busy and dynamic working environment of a school classroom and other educational settings.

Stage six: Use the analysis of your evidence to evaluate your practice and identify ways in which it might be developed to have a more positive impact on the outcomes for the learners. In Chapter 9, we will discuss the value of this 'real-time' evaluation and how this can be used to understand how an individual teacher's practice can be developed to have greater impact on learners' progress.

Stage seven: Implement the changes you have identified and return to stage five. Continue this reflective cycle for as long as you need to feel confident of having made good progress with the identified aspect of your teaching.

That all sounds very neat and tidy but the reality of action research is often rather 'messy', as it is undertaken in a dynamic context with living, breathing participants and you are a living, breathing researcher whose main challenge is to fulfil the role of the teacher, as well as undertake research. This means that the neat and tidy cycle of action research is often much more chaotic than it might appear at first.

WHERE ACTION RESEARCH 'FITS' IN THE WORLD OF EDUCATION RESEARCH

There are various different approaches to research in the field of education, and it is helpful to know where action research 'fits' in this broad range, as this helps to define both what it is and what it is not, which we will explore further later in this chapter.

KINDS OF KNOWLEDGE

Different kinds of research are underpinned by different ways of thinking about how we know what we know.

CRITICAL TASK 1.1

Have a look at the following questions. For each one, think about *how you know* what you know.

- What day is it today?
- Is smoking bad for you?
- What is money?
- How are you feeling just now?
- What shape is the Earth?
- What country are you in?
- What is learning?

Looking across all your answers, do these represent similar or different kinds of knowledge?

When talking about the nature of their research and the contribution that they hope it will make, researchers often use three key words to help them describe their own position in relation to knowledge: 'ontology', 'epistemology' and 'paradigm'.

'Ontology' relates to the nature of knowledge, while 'epistemology' relates to how new knowledge is 'created'. As you reflected on the questions in Critical task 1.1, you may have considered that there are different kinds of knowledge, and how it is that this knowledge has been developed: some knowledge is based on evidence, some is subjective, some is based on accepted norms and some may be highly contested. For example, we can be fairly sure that smoking is bad for us, as this claim is supported by a large body of evidence, both about the effects of smoking on the human body and the increased likelihood of suffering ill health for people who smoke. On the other hand, days of the week are not 'real' but based on widely accepted cultural norms: Wednesdays do not actually exist, but it can be useful for the smooth functioning of society for us all to behave as if they do.

The word 'paradigm' refers to the 'world view', or set of beliefs about knowledge, that form the basis for a particular approach to research. There are several research paradigms so, for the purposes of providing an introduction, it is helpful to compare two that are contrasting: the 'positivist' and 'interpretivist' paradigms. In the positivist paradigm, a physicist examining the behaviour of a pendulum may believe that they will be able to arrive at an answer to a particular question, if they carefully collect and analyse the relevant data. They will strengthen their confidence in the answer by repeating the investigation and inviting others to reproduce the process, leading to similar results. On the other hand, in the interpretivist paradigm, a social science researcher who is trying to understand a particular aspect of human interaction will recognise that humans are all different and the way that they interact is complex and unpredictable. Any data that they gather might be interpreted in a number of different ways but helps to build an understanding or give an insight into complex social issues.

It is worth remembering, of course, that ontology, epistemology and paradigms are themselves human constructs and, as such, they not fixed, constant or beyond challenge. However, as Punch and Oancea (2014: 16) state, they can helpfully provide ways in which to talk about knowledge and some important aspects of research:

 Methods of inquiry are based on assumptions – assumptions about the nature of the reality being studied, assumptions about what constitutes knowledge of that reality, and assumptions about what therefore are appropriate ways (or methods) of building knowledge of that reality.

Table 1.1 gives a very brief comparison of the positivist and interpretivist paradigms.

Table 1.1   Research paradigms

	Positivist paradigm	**Interpretivist paradigm**
Ontology	Reality is out there	Reality is a social construct
Epistemology	Reality can be measured	Reality can be explored and is open to interpretation
Methodology	e.g. Scientific method	e.g. Action research
Type of data	Quantitative (numbers)	Qualitative (words)
Types of data collection method	Statistical measures, large surveys, randomised-control trials	Observations, reflective diaries, copies of documents
Approach to analysis	Clear answers to clear questions	Nuanced understandings of human behaviour and interactions
Perceptions of strengths/ limitations	HARD but details and nuance can be lost	SOFT but detailed and meaningful to the researcher

KINDS OF EDUCATION RESEARCH

These different ways of thinking about generating new knowledge are reflected in the wide range of approaches to educational research.

Some large-scale empirical studies adopt a quasi-scientific approach: they gather large amounts of data in order to answer specific questions about teaching approaches or factors that impact on learning. Some experimental approaches utilise randomised-control trials, in which participants are allocated randomly to receive different educational experiences so that the impact of different approaches to teaching can be 'compared'. Some large-scale research projects aim to make international comparisons. Probably the best known of these is the Programme for International Student Assessment (commonly known as PISA), which aims to compare the ability of 15-year-olds, across many countries, to apply their school-learning to real-life challenges.

Rather than generating their own new data, some researchers specialise in drawing together large amounts of existing data from other published research. These studies are often referred to as 'meta-analyses', as they aim to analyse and synthesise the findings already undertaken by other researchers. The Education Endowment Foundation (EEF) is one well-known publisher of meta-analyses and their *Teaching and Learning Toolkit* is a valuable, open-access resource that supports school leaders to understand the likely impact of various strategies for school improvement and how robust the evidence is to support each approach.

Action research is one approach within a range of small-scale practitioner studies. Many teachers and other educational professionals gather evidence about their immediate, day-to-day work, in order to understand a particular aspect of the running of the school or setting; for example, a headteacher might send a questionnaire to parents to ask for their views on the school's homework policy or a senior leader might observe how children use the playground, in order to help them decide on training requirements for lunchtime supervisors or which new equipment to order. Some teachers might work together to explore a key issue across a school or cluster of schools; for example, a whole subject department in a secondary school might all try a new approach to engaging children at the start of lessons and review this together to see how well it worked. While action research is also undertaken on a small scale by practitioners who are enquiring about their own practice, its distinctive features relate to the incremental and cumulative improvement of practice, through careful examination of evidence related to the quality of teaching and its impact on learning.

CRITICAL TASK 1.2

Every approach to educational research has its strengths and limitations. Have a look at Table 1.2, and think through some of the strengths and potential limitations for each kind of research. We'll give our own thoughts towards the end of the chapter.

Table 1.2   Strengths and potential limitations of different types of research

Type of research	Strengths	Potential limitations
Large-scale experimental research		
Meta-analyses		
Small-scale practitioner research		

SOME POSSIBLE CRITICISMS OF ACTION RESEARCH

It is important to acknowledge here that action research is open to criticism because of some of its key characteristics. In Table 1.3 we suggest some of its potential limitations, and some responses that demonstrate why it can be viewed as a valuable and worthwhile approach.

Table 1.3   Potential limitations of action research

Potential limitation	Response
Action research is weak due to its subjective nature, as the researcher is researching his or her own practice.	Good point. But action research is all about the researcher improving their practice as a teacher, not about 'proving' anything. However, it is important for the action researcher to ensure that their evidence is as robust and meaningful as possible. More on this in Chapter 6.
Action research relies, largely, on qualitative evidence and this is weak as it is open to interpretation.	All data, including quantitative, is open to interpretation. In the case of action research, the teacher wants to understand the detail of their practice and the detail of its impact on learning over short timescales, so quantitative data is unlikely to be useful. Qualitative data is often very rich and can yield meaningful insights into learning. However, the action researcher must take care that they interpret their evidence in a balanced way. More on this in Chapters 9 and 14.
Action research makes no real contribution to knowledge, as it is a fundamentally introspective activity.	Yes, that's right. The point of action research is to help a new teacher become better at teaching and, as such, it is a personal and reflective process. It is unlikely the action researcher will discover something genuinely 'new'.
Research undertaken by just one teacher in one school or setting has low reliability: the findings can't be applied anywhere else.	Yes, it is true that research carried out by an individual teacher is not going to be highly reliable (more on the definition of this in Chapter 6), but the findings may well have a resonance for other teachers, as there may be elements they recognise from their own teaching. The action researcher should aim to ensure their evidence is robust and meaningful in their context. More on this in Chapter 6.

WHAT ACTION RESEARCH IS NOT: COMMON PITFALLS

Action research is sometimes misunderstood, possibly because the term itself is not exactly a 'does what it says on the tin' type of phrase and is open to interpretation. In the list below, we provide responses to some common alternative conceptions or questions that new and aspiring teachers often raise about the nature of action research.

- 'So, I need to try out two or three approaches and then compare them to see which is best?' No. Just do your best teaching, in line with policies in the school or setting, and identify, through evidence-based evaluation, how you might develop some aspects of your teaching to have more impact on learning.
- 'But how will I prove that the teaching approach I choose is the best?' You won't. With action research, the aim is not to 'prove' that your teaching is fantastic, but to 'improve' your teaching, through evidence-based evaluation.
- 'Do I need to radically change my practice or the established practice in school to see what happens?' No. A key principle of action research is that you should do your 'best' teaching at all times and that you should not conduct 'experiments' to 'see what happens'. Think evolution rather than revolution.
- 'If the school where I am on placement or where I work already has a good system for x, how am I supposed to improve it?' To return to an important point: as the song goes, 'it ain't what you do, it's the way that you do it, and that's what gets results'. A system is just a system and 10 teachers could use the same system in 10 different ways: it is very often some small and subtle aspects of how we do what we do that make a significant difference to outcomes for learners.
- 'So, action research is about demonstrating improvement in practice? Should I start my project with some pretty poor teaching so that I can show how much I have improved over time?' Absolutely not. Remember to do your best teaching at all times.

CRITICAL TASK 1.3

James is in the final placement of his secondary science Postgraduate Certificate in Education (PGCE) course. Things are generally going well but James is becoming increasingly aware that he tends to dominate the learning going on in his lessons: he asks most of the questions, the young people make very short responses and have very little opportunity to raise their own questions or identify topics for discussion and exploration. He is worried that, if he hands over too much control to the students, their behaviour might become more challenging, but he can't shake the feeling that the balance of intellectual activity is not how he would like it to be. What should James do next?

SKILLS AND ATTRIBUTES NEEDED BY TEACHERS UNDERTAKING ACTION RESEARCH

There are a number of skills and attributes that are needed when undertaking action research:

- Be committed to developing and improving your own practice: this is perhaps the most important attribute that you will need. All teachers need to meet the *Teachers' Standards* (DfE, 2012) in order to be awarded Qualified Teacher Status (QTS) and the *Teachers' Standards* are often, therefore, an excellent starting point for identifying a focus (more on that in Chapter 2), but there is often something more fundamental that drives most teachers: a desire for all children to make as much progress as possible in all of their lessons, or, as Sagor and Williams (2017: 13) describe it, 'universal student success'. Children's success, or progress, is dependent on the quality of your teaching, so if you are striving to maximise children's progress, you must also strive to improve your teaching.
- Be realistic: as we have already said, you are not seeking to prove anything. Your action research is highly unlikely to change the world, but it should help you improve your teaching. Even then, it is likely that there will still be room for further improvement. Remember that you will be focusing on a very specific aspect of your teaching, so even when you have improved in that particular area, there will be other aspects of your practice that can be improved. Teaching is complex and multifaceted.
- Be organised: perhaps this goes without saying, as all teachers, whether new or aspiring, or more experienced, need to be very organised anyway. However, remember that you will be carrying out action research as part of your teaching, not as a separate project, so this increases the need for you to be very well organised, if you are going to manage teaching and collecting data at the same time.
- Be able to prioritise: as we have just mentioned, your research will be part of your teaching, but it is crucial that you always put the children's needs first, so your research may, on occasion, need to 'take a back seat'. We will discuss the ethical considerations of undertaking action research in Chapters 5 and 7.
- Be able to remain focused: teachers are usually utilising many of their teaching skills simultaneously in any teaching and learning situation, so, when collecting data and evaluating, it can be easy to become sidetracked and collect data that is not relevant to your focus or to reflect on other aspects of your practice. Staying focused will not only ensure that you are more likely to achieve the objectives for your enquiry, it will also make the whole process more manageable. There is lots of advice in this book to help you to remain focused, particularly in Chapters 2, 3, 8 and 9.
- Be observant: whether or not you are using observation as a source of data (more on this in Chapter 6), it is important that you remain observant throughout. From noticing children's verbal and non-verbal responses in a particular situation, to spotting a 'critical moment' that illustrates the relationship between your teaching and the children's learning, teachers undertaking action research need to be constantly alert and recognise what is significant and relevant to their research focus (Roberts-Holmes, 2018).

- Be objective, open, honest: as identified in Table 1.3, the approach of the researcher is very important in managing any of the potential limitations of action research. You need to be honest and seek to avoid any preconceived ideas as you analyse and reflect on the data, so that you are open to 'seeing the unexpected' (Howells and Gregory, 2016: 96). The first bullet point in this list is 'commitment to improving your practice'; if you are genuinely committed to this, you must be willing to consider multiple possibilities, even if they are not what you are hoping for. Standing back and reflecting openly and critically is crucial. You can read more about this, including the possible use of a 'critical friend' to help you consider other perspectives, in Chapter 9.

HOW TO USE THIS BOOK

The book is structured into three parts that reflect the chronology of undertaking an action research project. Broadly, you should refer to Part 1 before starting your action research project, Part 2 while engaged in the process of gathering and reflecting on evidence, and Part 3 if you want (or need) to write up your project as a report. The three parts and their constituent chapters are outlined here.

PART 1: PLANNING AND PREPARING FOR YOUR ACTION RESEARCH PROJECT

Part 1 will focus on all the preparatory activities that a new or aspiring teacher needs to undertake and the issues they will have to consider before getting started on their action research project. In this part, chapters will guide the reader through their preparations for a successful project.

CHAPTER 2: IDENTIFYING A FOCUS FOR YOUR ACTION RESEARCH PROJECT

This chapter will provide guidance on identifying an appropriate focus for your action research study and support in narrowing down the areas for development and providing a narrow context and focus for the study. Reference will be made to sources of evidence that you might draw on in deciding which area of your practice to focus on. Guidance will be included on the place of literature and, in particular, published meta-analyses of research into effective teaching, in order to help you identify areas of your practice for development.

CHAPTER 3: DEFINING CLEAR ENQUIRY OBJECTIVES

This chapter will provide practical advice about defining appropriate and clear enquiry objectives for the study which will help to ensure success throughout the process.

CHAPTER 4: ENGAGING WITH THE LITERATURE

This chapter will explore the importance of engaging with the published research and body of knowledge before undertaking the enquiry, and the significance of drawing on the established literature to inform practice and improvement in practice. Again, reference will be made to published meta-analyses of research into teacher effectiveness, including some that is easily accessible without reference to journal databases, such as the work by the Education Endowment Foundation (EEF). This chapter will support you in becoming critical when reading published research about 'what works' in teaching and learning, as educational contexts are too complex for simplistic judgements about effective practice.

CHAPTER 5: CONSIDERING ETHICAL ISSUES

Ethical issues will be considered in some depth and in a practical way, as these are often either over-complicated or under-emphasised; in action research, the non-contentious nature of the enquiries can lead to a rather *laissez-faire* approach and student teachers require clear guidance on what is appropriate.

CHAPTER 6: PLANNING TO GATHER DATA

In this chapter, consideration will be given to the active planning required for gathering good quality and meaningful data which could be useful to evaluate the impact of teaching on children's learning. There will be an emphasis on the benefits of qualitative evidence and the limitations of quantitative evidence in small-scale projects.

PART 2: UNDERTAKING YOUR ACTION RESEARCH PROJECT

Part 2 is designed to provide a reference point for student teachers while on teaching practice, or new teachers embarking on an action research project, to guide them in what they should be doing and thinking about to enable them to get the most out of their project. It will therefore return to many of the issues addressed in Part 1, but with a focus on action rather than planning.

CHAPTER 7: ETHICS IN ACTION

This chapter will return to the issue of ethics to provide a checklist of issues to be addressed early in the placement, and gives further consideration to some of the subtle ethical issues that might arise, in the early stages of the project, in relation to issues such as informed consent and equitable treatment of all children, as well as the need to abide by schools' child protection policies and ensure the welfare of vulnerable children.

CHAPTER 8: 'CAPTURING' YOUR EVIDENCE

This chapter will give consideration to the importance of 'capturing' evidence, particularly as much rich evidence is 'transient' and can easily slip away during the course of a busy school day. The chapter will provide guidance on how to stay focused and the potential benefits of taking an iterative approach so that changes in the focus and methods can be adopted.

CHAPTER 9: EVALUATING AS YOU GO

This chapter will encourage new and aspiring teachers to evaluate on a regular basis, as they go, rather than waiting until the end of the placement to review all the evidence. Guidance will be given on how to 'make sense' of evidence through focusing on detail and strengthening evaluation by reflecting on a range of sources of evidence.

PART 3: WRITING YOUR ACTION RESEARCH PROJECT REPORT

Part 3 will provide guidance on writing the project as a concise and evidence-rich dissertation or assignment. Throughout, this part will draw on examples to illustrate some of the points about effective writing.

CHAPTER 10: WRITING THE INTRODUCTION TO YOUR ACTION RESEARCH REPORT

This chapter will provide guidance on communicating a clear rationale for the enquiry and on how to decide which contextual information is important to include in the account. It will emphasise the need for alignment throughout the written report, based on clear and appropriate objectives.

CHAPTER 11: WRITING THE LITERATURE REVIEW

This chapter will help student teachers to understand how to engage critically with published research and other literature sources through exploring their validity and reliability or through comparing sources, and offers guidance on suitable structures for the review.

CHAPTER 12: WRITING THE ENQUIRY DESIGN OR RESEARCH PLAN

This chapter will provide guidance on how to succinctly present an appropriate enquiry design, focusing closely on the specific approaches taken to gather and interpret evidence, with consideration of their potential strengths and limitations, and with appropriate reporting of the management of ethical issues.

CHAPTER 13: WRITING THE IMPLEMENTATION AND ANALYSIS SECTION

This chapter will provide guidance on how to write an evidence-rich, analytical, evaluative and concise account of the enquiry and how tentative conclusions can be drawn. The emphasis will be on the need for self-criticality in order to improve teaching.

CHAPTER 14: WRITING THE CONCLUSION TO YOUR ACTION RESEARCH REPORT

This chapter will provide guidance on how to write a clear and effective summary to the written report, with consideration of how to summarise findings and reflect on the relative strengths and limitations of the study.

The three main parts of the book should not be seen as entirely separate as some student teachers may undertake some writing of their project as they go along or even before the placement or project begins, and there is clearly some interplay between preparations before the project and actions undertaken during it. The book will finish with a conclusion (Chapter 15), which will include some general guidance on how to write well and how to avoid some common errors in academic writing. Throughout the book, there are case studies and critical tasks for consideration, to help clarify the issues and to explore the themes more fully. Suggested 'answers' to some of these are provided at the end of each chapter.

RESPONSE TO CRITICAL TASK 1.2

In this task, we asked you to think through some of the strengths and potential limitations for different kinds of research in education. In Table 1.4 we give some of our own thoughts.

(Continued)

Table 1.4   Answers to strengths and potential limitations of different types of research

Type of research	Strengths	Potential limitations
Large-scale experimental research	This kind of research can be useful to establish 'what works' in teaching and learning.	Things that 'work' in research studies don't always translate well to working in the real world.
Meta-analyses	It is valuable to see how much confidence can be placed in findings that are replicated in various studies.	Much of the detail of individual studies is lost. It's often the detail that helps practitioners apply research findings in practice.
Small-scale practitioner research	The research can have high value and meaning to those involved, as it relates directly to their work.	The research has limited applicability to anyone not directly involved.

RESPONSE TO CRITICAL TASK 1.3

James is in the final placement of his secondary science PGCE course and is becoming increasingly aware that he tends to dominate the learning going on in his lessons and he can't shake the feeling that the balance of intellectual activity is not how he would like it to be. What should James do next?

James has identified a mismatch between what he believes about teaching and learning and what this 'looks like' in his lessons: this is an excellent starting point for an action research enquiry. Having identified this as a potential problem, he might do a number of useful things:

- read about some practical and realistic ways in which he might hand some of the intellectual control over to his students. For example, Forster and Penny (2020) suggest that science teachers should try to reduce the number of questions they ask in their lessons and encourage children and young people to raise their own scientific questions
- consider how he could evaluate his own questioning and the impact of this on learning in his lessons
- read about some practical and realistic ways in which he might hand some of the intellectual control over to his students
- begin to identify an approach that he could take to have some positive impacts on the young people's abilities to raise their own scientific questions.

SUMMARY FOR THIS CHAPTER

In this chapter, we have established the nature of action research as a research methodology. We have considered how it can provide a useful framework for new and aspiring teachers to focus on improving their practice through evidence-based evaluation. Evidence is central to action research as it provides the basis for analysis and claims about the effectiveness of teaching, through examining its impact on learning, which can lead to action for developing teaching and improving outcomes for children. We have noted the skills and attributes required of teachers undertaking action research and identified some different ways in which researchers think about knowledge creation and some different kinds of education research, all of which has helped to define both what action research is and what it is not. In Part 1, we will begin to consider in more detail the preparations that will support a highly effective action research project. We end this chapter with a list of dos and don'ts for you to bear in mind as you read later chapters. Similar lists will appear throughout the book.

Do:

- think of action research as a way to evaluate and improve your own practice
- remember, 'it ain't what you do, it's the way that you do it' that gets results
- keep in mind the need for evidence to form the basis for rigorous evaluation
- remember that action research is 'messy'
- keep reading if you want to become a better teacher.

Don't:

- think that action research will enable you to 'compare' teaching and learning approaches or 'prove' which is best
- keep reading if you want to undertake experimental studies into teaching and learning.

FURTHER READING

The following sources may also support you in developing your understanding of action research:

Koshy, V. (2010) *Action Research for Improving Educational Practice*. 2nd edn. London: Sage.

This very readable book provides a clear introduction to the nature of processes involved in undertaking an action research enquiry and includes references to other sources, including relevant websites.

McNiff, J. (2017) *Action Research: All You Need to Know*. London: Sage.

McNiff is recognised as an expert in the field of action research and this helpful book provides an excellent introduction to the methodology.

Thomas, G. (2017) *How to Do Your Research Project: A Guide for Students*. 3rd edn. London: Sage.

This book provides a very clear and readable guide to the entire research process.

PART 1

PLANNING AND PREPARING FOR YOUR ACTION RESEARCH PROJECT

In Part 1, we explore the issues that should be considered before undertaking an action research project and the preparation that will help to ensure that the project is successful. The chapters included in Part 1 are:

Chapter 2: Identifying a focus for your action research project. This chapter provides guidance on identifying an appropriate focus for an action research study and advice on how to consider a range of possible areas for development before identifying a narrow context and focus for the study. Reference is made to the *Teachers' Standards* (DfE, 2012) and other sources of evidence that new and aspiring teachers might draw on in deciding which area of their practice to focus on. Guidance is included on the place of literature and, in particular, published meta-analyses of research into effective teaching, in order to help the new or aspiring teacher identify areas of their practice for development.

Chapter 3: Defining clear enquiry objectives. This chapter provides practical advice about defining appropriate and clear enquiry objectives for the study which will help to ensure success throughout the process.

Chapter 4: Engaging with the literature. This chapter explores the importance of engaging with the published research and body of knowledge before undertaking a professional enquiry, and the significance of drawing on the established literature to inform practice and improvement in outcomes for learners. Again, reference is made to published meta-analyses of research into teacher effectiveness, including some that is easily accessible without reference to journal databases, such as work by the Education Endowment Foundation. This chapter aims to support new and aspiring teachers in becoming critical when reading published research about 'what works' in teaching and learning, as educational contexts are too complex for simplistic judgements about effective practice.

Chapter 5: Considering ethical issues. In this chapter, ethical issues are considered in some depth and in a practical way, as these are often either over-complicated or under-emphasised. In action research, the non-contentious nature of the enquiries can lead to a rather *laissez-faire* approach, and this chapter aims to support new and aspiring teachers in understanding the practical steps that they can take to ensure that their work is ethically sound.

Chapter 6: Planning to gather data. In this chapter, consideration is given to the active planning required for gathering good quality and meaningful data which could be useful to evaluate the impact of teaching on children's learning. There is an emphasis on the potential benefits of qualitative evidence, and the associated limitations of quantitative evidence, in small-scale projects. The chapter aims to support new and aspiring teachers in making successful plans to gather good data to ensure that their analysis and evaluation can be evidence-based and meaningful.

2

IDENTIFYING A FOCUS FOR YOUR ACTION RESEARCH PROJECT

OBJECTIVES FOR THIS CHAPTER

- To explore the principles underpinning the identification of a suitable focus for an action research project
- To consider the range of evidence about personal professional priorities which might inform the process of identifying a suitable focus
- To consider how a broad focus can be narrowed to form the basis for a manageable project
- To explore some examples of foci which are 'action researchable' (and some which are not).

GETTING STARTED ON IDENTIFYING A FOCUS

In this chapter, we will consider how you might select an appropriate focus for your action research enquiry. As we established in Chapter 1, the key purpose of action research is to improve and develop your professional practice as a teacher, in order to enable the children and young people you work with to make good progress in their learning, and this should be the guiding principle for identifying a focus. As identified by Koshy (2010), this very early and important stage of your study can be challenging, so it is useful to review some key sources of evidence that might inform the process of identifying a suitable focus.

PREVIOUS FEEDBACK FROM OTHERS (RELATED TO THE *TEACHERS' STANDARDS*)

As you train to teach, and during the early stages of your teaching career, you will receive feedback on your practice from more experienced professionals, which should help you to identify your strengths and some areas for development, in relation to the *Teachers' Standards*. This feedback can sometimes seem overwhelming, as the process of becoming an outstanding teacher is complex and challenging, so it is worth reviewing, in a balanced way, to see whether there are any recurring themes or issues that might enable you to take steps towards becoming a great teacher. If so, it may be that one of these might usefully form the basis for your enquiry.

SELF-EVALUATION IN RELATION TO THE *TEACHERS' STANDARDS*

Self-evaluation is central to the development of great teachers and you have probably been engaging in some explicit self-evaluation throughout your training programme. In reviewing the *Teachers' Standards* on a weekly basis, you may have identified some that are your natural strengths and some that are more challenging, perhaps because of your previous experience or because some standards are multifaceted and some seem to become more complex the more you understand them. If, through self-evaluation, you can identify one or two aspects of your practice that you would like to improve or develop then you are well on your way towards identifying a suitable focus for your enquiry.

'GAPS ANALYSIS' IN RELATION TO THE *TEACHERS' STANDARDS*

Another approach to reflecting on your progress towards meeting the *Teachers' Standards* is through a 'gaps analysis'. Over the course of a school experience placement, you may have the opportunity to gain experience in relation to many of the standards, and you are likely to keep some records of your progress. These can provide a useful point for reflection in identifying those areas of the standards that have proved difficult to gain experience in or in which you feel you have not had much opportunity to make progress. Again, if you can identify an aspect of your practice that is, for whatever reason, somewhat 'under-developed', this may well be useful in identifying a suitable focus for your enquiry.

HIGHER-ORDER TEACHING SKILLS, WITH REFERENCE TO THE *TEACHERS' STANDARDS*

In order to improve your teaching, you may wish to focus on those aspects of your practice that will help you progress from being a satisfactory teacher to being a good teacher, or from being a good teacher to being a very good teacher. Many teacher training courses make use of grade or level descriptors and these can help you to identify the 'next steps' you should take on your way to becoming the best teacher you can be and, as such, might also form the basis for a suitable enquiry focus.

HIGH-IMPACT TEACHING SKILLS, WITH REFERENCE TO APPROPRIATE RESEARCH RELATED TO THE *TEACHERS' STANDARDS*

Whether or not your programme uses level or grade descriptors, there is a wealth of research evidence that may be useful to inform your thinking about which aspects of your practice could be developed to have a significant impact on the outcomes for the children or young people you teach. For example, the Black Box reports, starting with *Inside the Black Box* by Black and Wiliam (1990), provide teachers with robust evidence that engaging children in a positive and developmental assessment process has a demonstrable impact on their progress. Similarly, the Education Endowment Foundation (www.educationendowment-foundation.org.uk) provides easily accessible research information about aspects of practice that research suggests are likely to have the greatest impacts on progress and learning. It may be very useful to inform your reflections about identifying a suitable focus for your enquiry by engaging with the available research, so that you can tailor your approach to achieve a great impact on the learning of the children or young people you teach.

A PROFESSIONAL ISSUE THAT HAS PIQUED YOUR INTEREST AND THAT RELATES DIRECTLY TO YOUR PRACTICE

Finally, it may be that there has been a professional issue related to teaching and learning which has piqued your interest and motivated you to find out more and may act as a catalyst to develop your practice. It may be, for example, that an issue discussed in a training session has challenged your thinking about an area of practice that you had not considered before, such as whether teachers ask too many questions and whether children are given sufficient thinking time to respond to questions. In using an 'interesting professional issue' as the starting point for an enquiry focus, it is important that you keep it closely related to your own professional practice.

Remember that action research is not about 'comparing' approaches or finding the 'best' approach or even 'proving' that an approach works. It is about improving your practice through evidence-based analysis about the quality of your teaching and its impact on the learning of the children or young people you teach.

It is sometimes difficult to take action on your targets all at once and a great benefit of action research is that it allows you to focus on developing one aspect of your practice at a time and to evaluate your progress in an evidence-based way.

CRITICAL TASK 2.1

Jane is a School Direct PGCE primary student about to embark on the final school placement of her course. Her grades and feedback from her previous placements suggest that she is doing well with most aspects of her teaching and that she has very good potential as a teacher. However, she has a lower grade related to embedding differentiation into her teaching and the placement report suggests that this should be a target for her future development, to ensure that she maximises learning opportunities for every child.

Based on this feedback, how might Jane go about identifying a suitable focus for an action research project?

NARROWING YOUR FOCUS

Once you have identified an area of your practice that you wish to develop, it is important to narrow your focus to make it both manageable and meaningful (Brown, 2019). As we shall discuss further in Chapter 6, it is easy to gather lots of potential 'evidence' about your teaching and the children's learning which may not be very useful. A narrow and well-defined focus and, as we shall discuss in Chapter 3, clear objectives will enable you to be very clear about what you are trying to achieve and the evidence you need to gather in order to do so, and will keep the project manageable.

Another reason to narrow your focus is because some aspects of teaching that are worthwhile and appropriate for an action research project are also very wide-ranging and potentially enormous in their scope. Take, for example, Assessment for Learning (AfL): this is a very worthwhile aspect of practice to develop as it is widely recognised as a set of higher-order teaching skills which will have a very significant impact on pupil progress. However, AfL is also huge, incorporating written feedback (either within the lesson or after the lesson), verbal feedback, self-assessment, peer-assessment, use of success criteria, use of plenaries, use of individual or small group learning conferences and more.

It is also useful to consider other ways to limit the scope of your study. For example, you could aim to contextualise your study in a particular curriculum area, such as science or geography (primary), or with a particular year group (secondary). This can be a useful way to ensure that you are not overwhelmed by trying to gather evidence in every lesson you teach, and gives a greater sense of focus within your research. Limiting your study in this way has another important benefit: it may enable you to plan time between each teaching episode for evidence-based reflection on your practice and provide an opportunity for tracking children's progress within a specific context on a regular basis over time.

CRITICAL TASK 2.2

Geoff is an early years practitioner who wants to improve his practice in engaging children in sustained shared thinking. He realises that this is a broad area of practice. How could he narrow this down to make it more focused and manageable?

SOME FOCI FOR PROJECTS WHICH ARE 'ACTION RESEARCHABLE' . . . AND SOME WHICH ARE BEST AVOIDED

Action research, in the way in which we have defined it in this book, is all about the development of personal, professional practice. This means that a project that is tightly focused on the development of a specific aspect of your teaching repertoire is likely to be 'action researchable'. However, when offered an opportunity to undertake 'school-based' research, some new or aspiring teachers start their thinking with some project foci that are not action researchable or some that can become action researchable if given an 'action research (AR) tweak'. So, in the final section of this chapter, we will explore some examples of foci that are definitely action researchable, some that are best avoided and some that can be given an AR tweak to make them suitable foci.

SOME EXAMPLES OF ACTION RESEARCHABLE FOCI

❝ How can I develop my practice in AfL to enable children to make good progress? ❞

Although this question still requires some work to tighten it in terms of the specific aspect of AfL and subject or year group context, the central question is definitely action researchable, as it is closely related to the development of an aspect of practice which is likely to have a positive impact on the learning of the children or young people.

> I'd like to get better at my questioning, within History, to develop children's use of evidence as the basis for inferential thinking.

This focus is action researchable as it is closely bound to a specific aspect of practice and there is a clear expectation that the teacher's development in this skill will have a positive impact on the children's learning of historical skills. This focus might well have been influenced by a training experience that has inspired the new or aspiring teacher to develop their practice in a positive way and to master a higher-order teaching skill.

> I want to develop my skills in conversation with reception-age children to promote sustained shared thinking.

This example has a clear focus in relation to the practitioner's professional skills and, again, a well-defined anticipated positive impact on the children's learning. This focus may have been informed by reference to research about the role of the early years teacher in mastering the art of joining rather than dominating young children's interactions.

> How can I gain a better insight into children's scientific ideas and make more effective use of these in my lessons to promote scientific learning?

This focus is action researchable as it has a clear focus on improving an aspect of practice to have a positive impact on the learning. This teacher may have learnt from practice that drawing out the learners' initial and developing ideas provides some valuable insights to inform planning and address misconceptions.

SOME EXAMPLES OF FOCI THAT ARE BEST AVOIDED

> What is the best way for children to improve their handwriting?

This is well beyond the scope of a small action research project. Any focus that starts with the words 'What is the best way . . .' is probably inappropriate for action research, as it suggests the need for a research process that will 'test' or 'compare' approaches, which is not the purpose of action research.

 Does playing Beethoven during independent work improve outcomes in mathematics?

This sounds like a 'pet project' and is, again, beyond the scope of a small-scale study. The bigger objection is that this project will not improve the teaching skill of the new or aspiring teacher (beyond knowing how to use the school sound system).

 What is the optimum classroom temperature?

There is probably an important issue here that someone should research . . . but not you, not now. Again, while it might be part of good practice to ensure that learners are physically and emotionally comfortable during lessons, the new or aspiring teacher will not develop any teaching skills through this project and it is therefore a wasted opportunity.

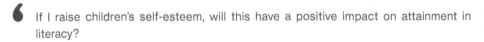

> If I raise children's self-esteem, will this have a positive impact on attainment in literacy?

This sounds like a very plausible and worthwhile focus for a study but is fraught with difficulty. There is clearly nothing wrong with positively supporting children's self-confidence, but gathering meaningful evidence about this and finding genuine correlation to an impact on attainment in literacy is likely to prove impossible.

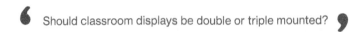

> Should classroom displays be double or triple mounted?

This is just bonkers.

SOME EXAMPLES OF FOCI THAT COULD BE GIVEN AN AR TWEAK

> Which is the best method for children to do self-assessment in mathematics?

In one sense, this is a very reasonable question but it is not, as it stands, appropriate for an action research project. However, with a little bit of refocusing and an AR tweak, this project could become a very worthwhile action research project. In general, in teaching, it's not *what* you do but *the way that you do it* that gets results, so there is no 'best method' for children to do self-assessment. The big challenge for us as teachers, and the factor that is likely to have an impact on outcomes, is how we engage the learners in the process. So, to make this into a worthwhile action research project, you might ask: 'How can I engage learners effectively in self-assessment to enable them to make good progress in mathematics?'

> Can circle time impact positively on children's behaviour in the playground?

Again, there is something worthwhile here, but it is not within the scope of a small-scale project. However, if you are keen to develop your practice in leading circle time sessions, this is a suitable focus and you could gather useful evidence about this aspect of your teaching and its impact on children's social and emotional learning within the classroom.

> How could I develop a whole-school policy on written feedback?

This is clearly an inappropriately over-ambitious project for a new or aspiring teacher. However, if you are keen to develop your own practice in providing meaningful written feedback that has a positive impact on learning then this can easily be given an AR tweak: 'How can I develop the quality of my written feedback, and increase children's engagement with it, to improve outcomes in science?' As we will go on to discuss in Chapter 14, sharing your findings with your colleagues can be a very valuable part of the process and it is possible that this may inform practice, and even policy, in the school more widely.

CRITICAL TASK 2.3

Table 2.1 has some questions for you to consider. For each one, decide whether it is action researchable, is best avoided or could become action researchable if given a suitable tweak.

Table 2.1   Identifying action researchable questions

	Action researchable	Not suitable for action research	Could be given a tweak to make it action researchable
What is the impact of using first-hand resources in history?			
Does wait-time increase the quality of children's verbal responses?			
Are open questions better than closed questions?			
Do children prefer stickers or stamps?			
Is ability-grouping effective?			
Is laminating resources a good use of tax-payers' money?			

RESPONSE TO CRITICAL TASK 2.1

Jane would like to develop her approach to differentiation to ensure all children make good progress. As differentiation is such a large area of practice, she would like to focus on just one aspect, such as her use of questioning, resourcing, the matching of tasks to learning, peer-supported learning or the allocation of appropriate adult support. She decides to contextualise her enquiry in science, as this will enable her to gather evidence from one or two lessons a week, to allow time for reflection and development, and to focus on differentiating how children record their learning of science.

RESPONSE TO CRITICAL TASK 2.2

Geoff would like to develop his practice in supporting sustained shared thinking in an early years setting. He decides that the key aspect of his practice that he needs to develop is the way in which he joins in children's conversations: he would like to reduce the tendency he has of 'taking over' and asking too many questions. He decides that he should contextualise his enquiry in children's outdoor learning, as this will give good opportunities for the kind of skills he wants to develop.

RESPONSE TO CRITICAL TASK 2.3

In Critical task 2.3, we asked you to consider some questions and decide whether each one is action researchable, best avoided or action researchable if given a suitable tweak. In Table 2.2, we have presented our own responses to these questions.

Table 2.2 Identifying action researchable questions (revisited)

	Action researchable	Not suitable for action research	Could be given a tweak to make it action researchable
What is the impact of using first-hand resources in history?			Focus on how you can utilise resources effectively to support learning.
Does wait-time increase the quality of children's verbal responses?			This is already widely accepted, so the focus is on how you engage children through your questioning.
Are open questions better than closed questions?			Again, this is already widely accepted but it would be a great focus to develop the quality and impact of your questions.
Do children prefer stickers or stamps?		Best avoided. Answering this will not improve your teaching skills.	

	Action researchable	Not suitable for action research	Could be given a tweak to make it action researchable
Is ability-grouping effective?		Best avoided as this can't be answered in a small-scale project and it would be much better to focus on a key aspect of your teaching skills.	
Is laminating resources a good use of tax-payers' money?		Best avoided. For obvious reasons.	

SUMMARY FOR THIS CHAPTER

In this chapter, we have considered the importance of choosing a suitable focus for your action research project, one that relates very directly and purposefully to the development of a well-defined aspect of your teaching skills. Choose a focus that relates to your own teaching, does not involve conducting an experiment, and that is likely to have a good impact on the quality of teaching and learning in your classroom. Once you have identified a focus, refine it in terms of its scope and context so that it becomes tightly defined and manageable. In the next chapter, we will explore how to define clear objectives to guide the study.

Do:

- focus on an area of your practice you wish to develop
- use evidence about your own development targets to inform your thinking
- use evidence about high-impact teaching strategies to inform your thinking
- narrow down your study to make it focused and manageable.

Don't:

- pursue an area of 'interest' or focus on a 'problem' in the current education system which does not relate to developing your current practice
- set out to run an experiment or to compare approaches or 'prove' that one approach is best
- be too ambitious
- worry about your title . . . we'll sort that out in Part 3.

FURTHER READING

The following sources may also support you in the process of identifying a focus:

Baumfield, V., Hall, E. and Wall, K. (2013) *Action Research in Education*. 2nd edn. London: Sage.

Chapter 3 of this text offers useful guidance in relation to identifying and refining a focus for an action research enquiry.

Hulse, B. and Hulme, R. (2012) 'Engaging with research through practitioner enquiry: the perceptions of beginning teachers on a postgraduate initial teacher education programme', *Educational Action Research*, 20 (2): 313–29.

This helpful article explores the perceptions of student teachers in relation to small-scale professional enquiry projects while on a one-year postgraduate initial teacher education programme. One particularly relevant finding is the view of some student teachers that a study is likely to be more successful if it is very focused, rather than exploring policy constraints that are beyond the scope of a small study by a new teacher.

Macintyre, C. (2000) *The Art of Action Research in the Classroom*. Abingdon: David Fulton Publishers.

This very clear and concise book includes a very helpful chapter on 'formulating a research question' that supports the identification of a clear and tight focus for an action research project.

3

DEFINING
CLEAR ENQUIRY
OBJECTIVES

OBJECTIVES FOR THIS CHAPTER

- To explore the purpose of enquiry objectives in keeping the enquiry focused and the difference between enquiry objectives and learning objectives
- To consider the relative merits of enquiry questions and objectives and the difference between the overarching aim of the project and the enquiry objectives
- To explore how objectives can be phrased to keep the enquiry focused and manageable as an action research project
- To explore some examples of objectives which are action researchable and some which are not.

ENQUIRY OBJECTIVES

In this chapter, we will consider how to create clear enquiry objectives that enable the action researcher to keep their project focused and purposeful throughout. Once an overarching aim has been identified, enquiry objectives should form a short set of clear statements that enable the researcher to be very clear about what he or she is trying to find out and can be referred to throughout the project. Action research can get messy and it is easy to lose sight of what you are trying to achieve, so the enquiry objectives provide a useful reference point at every stage of the process.

Lewis and McNaughton Nicholls (2014: 48) state that:

> A good research study is one which has a clearly defined purpose, in which there is coherence between the objectives, the research questions and the methods or approaches proposed, and which generates data which are meaningful, robust and relevant. It is also, importantly, one which is realistic.

This is good advice. It is important to keep your overarching aim in mind and to work from the focus for your enquiry to identify some tightly defined objectives. The overarching aim of the project will be to develop a particular aspect of your practice as a teacher, whereas the enquiry objectives will state clearly what you would need to find out in order to make evidence-based judgements about how you are getting on with that aspect of your practice and how you might improve it.

CRITICAL TASK 3.1

Remember Jane from the previous chapter? She was the School Direct PGCE primary student who wanted to develop her approach to differentiation, and decided to focus on children's recording in science lessons. Now that she has identified the overall aim and focus of her action research enquiry, she needs to identify some suitable objectives and she has asked for your help. Draft three or four objectives that you think would be useful to Jane in guiding her throughout the project.

HOW TO PHRASE YOUR OBJECTIVES AND SOME SUGGESTIONS OF WHAT TO AVOID

To keep your objectives useful throughout the project, you should aim to keep them tightly focused around what you would need to find out to make sound and valid judgements about the quality of your practice and the impact that your teaching is having on the children's learning. This dual focus, on both your teaching and the children's learning, should be reflected in your objectives and will enable you to understand and develop your practice over time.

You should avoid objectives that suggest that you plan to make a comparison of teaching methods or to find 'the best approach' to a particular aspect of teaching and learning. These objectives would normally be impossible to answer in a small-scale study and you should aim to keep your study focused on developing your practice rather than comparing approaches.

You should also avoid objectives that simply restate your overarching aim, such as 'To improve my questioning', as these do little to sharpen your focus on what you would need to know about your practice in order to improve it.

It is important to avoid confusing 'learning objectives' with 'enquiry objectives'. In planning for teaching and learning, we regularly use the word 'objective' and it is valuable for us to draw the distinction, at this point, between a learning objective and an enquiry objective. A learning objective relates to planning for learning and defines what it is that we intend children or young people to learn from a particular lesson or experience. In education action research, an enquiry objective relates to planning for our research and defines what it is that we need to 'find out' in order to understand and develop our practice.

Action research enquiry objectives should always start with the word 'To' and be followed by a suitably rigorous verb. Here are some examples:

To understand . . .

To analyse . . .

To evaluate . . .

To explore . . .

To identify . . .

To interrogate . . .

It is also useful to include the word 'impact' in at least one of your objectives, as a clear reminder that the effectiveness of teaching can only be judged in relation to its impact on learning. This, in turn, will guide you towards gathering evidence about both your teaching and the learning of the children or young people in your class, which we will discuss further in Chapter 6.

There is some debate about the relative merits of enquiry questions and enquiry objectives and which you choose is a matter of personal preference. While some authors, including Thomas (2017) and McNiff (2016b), refer more commonly to enquiry questions, we tend to recommend the use of objectives, as there is more potential to make mistakes in formulating enquiry questions than in formulating enquiry objectives. For example, a common mistake in the use of enquiry questions is to ask a question that invites a 'Yes or No' response, which can be limiting. However, with care, enquiry questions can be formulated that are just as effective as objectives, and Thomas (2017) recommends returning regularly to research questions to refine them to ensure they are tightly phrased and reflect the intention of the researcher.

CRITICAL TASK 3.2

Table 3.1 contains a selection of enquiry questions. What are the potential problems with these and how might they be improved or converted to objectives?

Table 3.1   Assessing enquiry questions

Enquiry question	Potential problems and suggested improvements
Can I improve my use of questioning to enhance young people's higher-order thinking skills?	
Does engaging children in self-assessment impact positively on their progress in writing?	
To what extent can children's historical understanding be developed through effective use of resources?	
Which is the best approach to teach children thinking skills in science?	

SOME ENQUIRY OBJECTIVES WHICH ARE 'ACTION RESEARCHABLE' . . . AND SOME WHICH ARE BEST AVOIDED

In the previous chapter, we identified the importance of defining a focus or overarching aim for your enquiry that is clearly related to improving your own professional practice, and we considered some examples of foci that are 'action researchable', some that could be given a tweak to make them action researchable, and some that are probably best avoided. This same principle follows through to the creation of enquiry objectives and, in this section, we explore some objectives that are action researchable, some that could be worthwhile with a little re-working and a few that are best avoided.

SOME EXAMPLES OF ACTION RESEARCHABLE ENQUIRY OBJECTIVES

A student teacher wants to improve their questioning and sets the following objectives:

1.   To examine the impact of my questioning on children's verbal responses in geography.
2.   To evaluate the quality of my questioning in geography.

The first is a suitable objective for an action research enquiry as it reminds the student teacher that they are not just evaluating the quality of their questions, but are doing so through seeking to understand the impact their questions are having on the children's thinking as demonstrated through their verbal responses. The second objective reminds the student teacher to gather evidence about the quality of their questioning, perhaps through seeking feedback from experienced teaching colleagues, or through comparing the phrasing of their questions to those suggested through published research. In both cases, the objectives will be appropriate throughout the stages of their enquiry: as they seek to improve their questioning over time, they will want to judge this in relation to the quality or phrasing of their questions and the nature of the children's responses.

EXAMPLE OF AN ENQUIRY QUESTION THAT IS BEST AVOIDED

A student teacher undertaking a PGCE in secondary history is interested in differentiation and sets the following enquiry question:

> Does the use of mixed ability grouping have a positive impact on the young people's learning in GCSE history lessons?

The student teacher is clearly keen to develop their approach to differentiation in order to meet the learning needs of all young people within the class, and they are thinking broadly about how they might achieve this, from teaching strategies to student groupings. However, this objective is not appropriate for action research, for two reasons: firstly, it sounds like it might involve a 'test' in which to compare the benefits of ability or mixed-ability groupings, and secondly, it does not focus on the development of a teaching skill, which is central to action research. Deciding how to group the children is certainly part of the teacher's role but, once it has been done, there is no further teaching skill to be developed.

SOME EXAMPLES OF ENQUIRY OBJECTIVES THAT COULD BE GIVEN AN AR TWEAK

A student teacher undertaking a primary PGCE is interested in developing their practice in engaging children in the assessment for learning process and has formulated the objective:

> To examine pupils' changing attitudes in response to my verbal feedback.

This student teacher has understood that a significant aspect of learning relates to the children's emotional response to learning situations and that feedback can be especially powerful in its impact on both positive and negative attitudes to learning. However, this objective has some limitations and would benefit from some re-working. It appears to be based on an assumption that the children or young people may have pre-existing negative attitudes in relation to verbal feedback, and the implication here is that the student teacher is 'not impressed' with the practice they have seen in school, and that they hope to do a better job themselves. Remember that it is not ethical to make judgements about the practice of others and, while action research is all about self-improvement, it should not be about setting out to be self-congratulatory. It would also be beneficial for this objective to be refocused towards learning rather than attitude, as it is, ultimately, the learning that is important and the acid test of the quality of teaching. It would also be beneficial to define the subject context more tightly. So, this objective could be tweaked from:

> To examine changing attitudes in response to my verbal feedback

to:

> To understand how children respond to my verbal feedback in Y3 mathematics lessons.

The same student teacher has developed another potential objective that would benefit from an AR tweak:

> To explore children's and teachers' views of assessment for learning.

While assessment for learning is a suitable focus for action research, the phrasing of this objective suggests that the student teacher wants to explore opinions about it, rather than focus on the development of their own practice. Assessment for learning is often a very good focus for action research, as embedding learner-centred approaches to assessment can have a very positive impact on progress, so it would be worthwhile for the student teacher to grapple with the wording of this objective, with a view to focusing on their own practice and what they would need to find out in order to develop and improve their use of formative assessment. So, this objective could be tweaked from:

To explore children's and teachers' views of assessment for learning

to:

To analyse the impact of my verbal feedback on children's progress in Y3 mathematics lessons.

STAYING FOCUSED BUT FLEXIBLE

Throughout your action research study, it is important to stay focused but, also, to be ready to take a flexible and responsive approach. Setting clear enquiry objectives is important in keeping a focused approach to the enquiry but, once established, these do not have to stay the same throughout the project. Taking an iterative approach will enable you to refine your objectives and, if need be, to change them quite significantly in response to a change in circumstances within the learning environment or a change in the overall focus of the enquiry. As McNiff and Whitehead (2005: 26) identify, 'often things do not go according to plan, because we are all free and unpredictable humans and do not always do as expected'. Be prepared to manage changes by regularly reviewing your enquiry objectives, to see whether you are veering away from your original focus or to identify ways in which your original objectives might need to be amended in the light of how things are going.

CRITICAL TASK 3.3

Table 3.2 has a selection of enquiry objectives to be improved. Consider how you could improve each objective to make it action researchable.

Table 3.2 Improving enquiry objectives

Objective	Potential problems and suggested improvements
To improve my use of questioning	
To establish whether open questions are more effective than closed questions	
To evaluate the children's skills in self-assessment	
To understand whether children who do not contribute in lessons learn as effectively as children who respond frequently	

RESPONSE TO CRITICAL TASK 3.1

Jane asked for your help in drafting some useful objectives for her enquiry focusing on meeting individual needs for children's learning in science through differentiating the recording of their learning. She is really keen to ensure that the recording should be part of the learning process and not just a dull chore. Possible objectives could include:

- to understand how the children engage with recording their science learning
- to analyse the impact of the children's recording on their science learning
- to evaluate my approach to engaging children in meaningful recording of their science learning.

RESPONSE TO CRITICAL TASK 3.2

In this critical task, you were invited to spot any potential problems with some enquiry questions and suggest ways they might be improved. Some possible responses are suggested in Table 3.3.

Table 3.3   Assessing enquiry questions (revisited)

Enquiry question	Potential problems and suggested improvements
Can I improve my use of questioning to enhance young people's higher-order thinking skills?	The main problem with this question is that the answer is going be either 'Yes' or 'No' and will probably be 'Yes'. The other potential problem is that the question is really a statement of the overarching aim of the enquiry and does not help the new or aspiring teacher to be clear about what they would need to find out or gather evidence about in order to understand how effective their questioning is and so consider how to improve it. So, a couple of possible objectives to be clear about this might be: <ul><li>to evaluate the questions I ask and how I ask them</li><li>to analyse the young people's responses, in order to understand the impact of my questions on their higher-order thinking skills.</li></ul>
Does engaging children in self-assessment impact positively on their progress in writing?	Again, the answer to this question is a binary 'Yes/No', and almost certainly 'Yes', as the principles of formative assessment are now widely accepted as being effective. Again, it does not help the new or aspiring teacher to identify what they would need to find out in order to understand their effectiveness in this area of their practice. So, some possible objectives might be: <ul><li>to understand how children engage in the self-assessment process</li><li>to analyse the impact of self-assessment on children's progress in writing</li><li>to evaluate how effectively I engage the children in the self-assessment process.</li></ul>

Enquiry question	Potential problems and suggested improvements
To what extent can children's historical understanding be developed through effective use of resources?	The use of the phrase 'To what extent' sounds like it may be better than the previous two examples, as it avoids a binary 'Yes/No' answer. However, it is an impossible question to answer and fails to establish clearly what the new or aspiring teacher needs to find out in order to improve their practice through evidence-based evaluation. So, some possible objectives might be: • to analyse the impact of my use of resources on children's understanding of chronology • to evaluate the effectiveness of my use of resources to enhance the children's historical understanding.
Which is the best approach to teaching children thinking skills in science?	This sounds like an experiment or a test and should be avoided. However, the sentiment is probably good, and, with some tweaks, this could form the basis of a worthwhile study, with some further focusing on a more specific aspect of practice. So, some possible objectives might be: • to understand the thinking skills that children use in my science lessons • to analyse the impact of my collaborative, problem-solving tasks on the children's thinking skills.

RESPONSE TO CRITICAL TASK 3.3

In this critical task, you were invited to spot any potential problems with some enquiry objectives and suggest some ways in which they might be improved. Some possible responses are suggested in Table 3.4.

Table 3.4 Improving enquiry objectives (revisited)

Objective	Potential problems and suggested improvements
To improve my use of questioning	This is a restatement of the overarching aim of the action research project. An objective should help me focus on what I need to understand to make a judgement about the quality of my questions, so some useful objectives might be: • to understand how children respond to my questions • to evaluate the quality of my questions • to analyse the impact of my questions on children's learning.

(Continued)

Table 3.4   (Continued)

Objective	Potential problems and suggested improvements
To establish whether open questions are more effective than closed questions	This has the makings of a test or experiment and it is already widely accepted that open questions promote richer thinking among learners. It sounds as though the student teacher's overarching aim is really to develop their use of questioning, including open questions, and, if so, the objectives from the example above might be suitable.
To evaluate the children's skills in self-assessment	This seems like it is not too bad . . . but the student teacher should ensure that their primary focus is the children's learning rather than their skills in self-assessment. That said, it is worth finding out how children respond to opportunities to self-assess, but it is the impact on learning that is most important, so perhaps the following objectives might be suitable: • to understand how children engage with the self-assessment process • to understand the impact of children's engagement with self-assessment on their progress in . . . • to evaluate my approach to engaging children in self-assessment.
To understand whether children who do not contribute in lessons learn as effectively as children who respond frequently	This one goes beyond the scope of an action research study and is very tricky. The student teacher probably wants to develop their skills in engaging all the children in the lesson through interactive teaching, which is a worthwhile goal, so objectives might be: • to understand how children engage in my lessons and identify any variability • to explore how children respond to my interactive teaching • to analyse the impact of my interactive teaching on children's learning in . . . • to evaluate my approach to engaging children to support their learning.

SUMMARY FOR THIS CHAPTER

In this chapter, we have considered the importance of establishing clear enquiry objectives that can guide you throughout your action research project. Enquiry objectives should be clear statements of what you need to find out in order to understand a specific aspect of your practice, the impact of that practice on the learners' progress or development, and what you can do to improve your teaching to have a greater impact on learning. Action research is an iterative process in which the focus and the objectives may change or be refined over time, so objectives should not be viewed as 'set in stone' and can be amended at almost any stage of the project.

Enquiry objectives keep us focused on 'what we need to find out' in order to make progress with our overarching aim for the project and, in Chapter 6, we will consider 'how to find out what we need to find out', through planning to gather the evidence that will support us in addressing the objectives. In the next chapter, we will explore the importance of informing the development of practice with reference to published research and other literature.

Do:

- choose either enquiry objectives or questions, not both (we favour enquiry objectives)
- keep them action researchable: stay focused on developing your practice
- keep them focused on what you need to find out in order to understand how you are doing with your overarching aim
- be prepared to give your objectives a tweak over time.

Don't:

- ask impossible questions
- confuse learning objectives and enquiry objectives
- set questions or objectives that aim to compare or ask 'which is best?'
- be too ambitious.

FURTHER READING

The following sources may also support you in defining clear objectives for your action research enquiry:

McNiff, J. (2016) *You and Your Action Research Project.* 4th edn. Abingdon: Routledge.

Part 3 of this significant text provides guidance on planning and managing an action research project.

Menter, I., Elliot, D., Hulme, M., Lewin, J. and Lowden, K. (2011) *A Guide to Practitioner Research in Education.* London: Sage.

Part 2 of this book is entitled 'What do we want to know?' and includes a chapter focusing on the formulation of relevant research questions. Although we recommend the use of enquiry objectives in preference to questions, the principles are the same for both processes.

Ritchie, J., Lewis, J., McNaughton Nicholls, C. and Ormston, R. (eds) (2014) *Qualitative Research Practice: A Guide for Social Science Students and Researchers.* London: Sage.

This comprehensive book frequently emphasises the need to keep all aspects of the research process well aligned to the overarching aim and the stated objectives.

ENGAGING WITH
THE LITERATURE

OBJECTIVES FOR THIS CHAPTER

- To consider the role of literature in preparing to undertake an action research project
- To explore the range of appropriate literature that might inform the development of practice through action research
- To consider how to read literature 'critically' and how to draw on the literature to provide a framework for evaluating practice.

READING BEFORE ACTION: THE ROLE OF LITERATURE

In this chapter, we will consider the role that literature will play in relation to your enquiry and explore how you can engage critically with the literature. The importance of engaging with literature at the early stages of the process cannot be overstated. Whether your enquiry will be written up, as an assignment or dissertation, or whether you just intend to carry out the enquiry to improve your practice, you will benefit greatly from engaging in some reading before starting the research, in relation to the two main aspects of methodology and practice.

LITERATURE ABOUT METHODOLOGY

Firstly, you need to engage with literature about the process of undertaking action research in the classroom. By reading this book, you have already embarked on this important step – well done.

As part of your engagement with literature about action research, you must ensure that you read about and understand the ethical implications of undertaking classroom-based research, so that you are able to consider and manage these within your own enquiry. The British Educational Research Association (BERA) publishes *Ethical Guidelines for Educational Research* (2018) on their website (www.bera.ac.uk) and this should be considered to be essential reading. There is more on ethical considerations and how to manage these in Chapters 5 and 7.

LITERATURE ABOUT PRACTICE

Given that the purpose of undertaking an action research process is to improve your practice, you should aim to engage with literature that will help you to identify the key issues relating to your focus and will inform your thinking as you seek to develop your practice. As has been established in Chapter 1, you will reflect on your practice and adapt it, through a cyclical approach; the reading that you undertake at an early stage in the process will develop your knowledge and understanding, so that the adaptations you make are more informed, rather than guessing at what might work. For example, if you decide to focus on developing your own questioning skills, you should aim to read about, and therefore develop your knowledge and understanding of, the key considerations involved in effective questioning, such as giving children time to think before answering, planning key questions in advance, types of question, and so on. Many people find it helpful to create a mind map or other visual representation of these key issues, so that, as they evaluate their developing practice and plan their next steps, they have something to refer back to and can decide what adaptations to make next. In the busyness of everyday teaching, time for reading 'in the moment' will be short, so it is important that you undertake as much reading as possible ahead of time.

CRITICAL TASK 4.1

Anna, a primary trainee teacher on a School Direct salaried route, is keen to focus on developing her approach to guiding pupils' self-reflection, having identified this through undertaking a 'gaps analysis' in relation to the *Teachers' Standards*, as suggested in Chapter 2. She has also followed the advice given about narrowing the focus of the enquiry and intends to base her project in her teaching of science. Anna is teaching in a Year 2 class and will be addressing the National Curriculum statutory requirements in relation to 'Plants'. Anna has never undertaken an action research enquiry previously. What advice would you give to Anna in terms of what she should aim to read about first?

EXPLORING RELEVANT LITERATURE

As has been identified above, it is important to read about the nature and process of action research in the classroom, including the ethical implications of undertaking such an enquiry. This book is intended to provide you with the necessary information, but there are also other key texts which focus on action research in education, such as those referred to in the further reading at the end of this and other chapters, and these should be relatively easy to locate within any academic library.

Identifying potential literature sources in relation to your focus, and deciding which to read, is more complex. It is important to read as widely as possible, both to develop your knowledge and understanding and to support you in reading critically (which will be explored later on in this chapter). However, you also need to be practical; with a busy schedule, it is likely that you will have limited time available for reading, so it is therefore important to remain focused.

While, as advised in Chapter 2, it is important to narrow your focus, perhaps by contextualising your study in a specific subject in primary (as Anna has done in Critical task 4.1), with a particular year group or class in secondary, or in relation to one aspect of a particular early learning goal in early years, this can lead to an initial struggle to identify sources of literature. For example, you may well find it difficult to identify sources that explicitly relate to making effective use of success criteria to support the development of reception-age children's ability to identify similarities and differences in relation to places. You will, however, be able to find literature sources that include the effective use of success criteria to support learning and teaching. You will be able to find literature sources that focus on effective practice in the Foundation Stage more generally. You will also be able to find literature sources that focus on effective pedagogy when teaching young children about 'place'. It can be helpful to think about this in terms of a Venn diagram, with the section where all sets overlap being the section most relevant to your enquiry, but the section where you are likely to find the least in the way of literature. You should aim to read in relation to each set of the Venn diagram, with greatest emphasis placed on your selected focus (effective use of success criteria, in the example above).

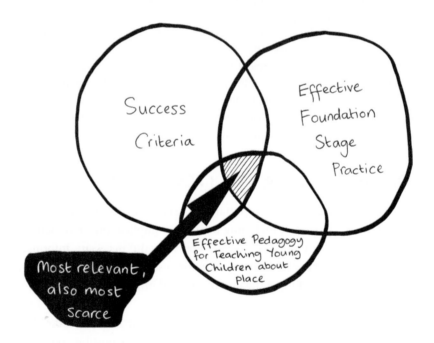

It is easy to start with sources that confirm 'why' your focus is relevant and valuable, such as Department for Education and Ofsted publications, particularly where these relate to current policy. This is a reasonable place to start, not least because such sources are freely available on the internet; as will be discussed in Chapter 10, you will need to provide a rationale for the selection of your focus, so these sources, together with reference to relevant *Teachers' Standards*, will be useful in supporting your justification. However, these are unlikely to focus on 'how' to develop your practice in the area that you have selected, so it is important to avoid spending too much time on reading that simply justifies your selection of focus.

If you have access to an academic library, there will undoubtedly be literature sources relevant to your focus and the subject in which you have chosen to contextualise your enquiry in the form of books on the shelves, or e-books available to read electronically.

If, for example, your focus is the effective use of differentiation to meet individual needs, there is likely to be a wealth of generic professional studies texts, most of which will include some advice in relation to differentiating effectively. Later in this chapter, we will consider the value of such 'advice' in relation to your enquiry. If you have chosen to contextualise your enquiry in your teaching of music with a class of Year 8 pupils, there will likely be some sources relating to the pedagogy of teaching music in secondary schools. If you are struggling to find them, most academic libraries have an electronic search facility for their texts; these will differ between institutions, so we will not offer advice on their use here, but suggest that you ask a librarian for help if you are unsure. There may be a designated education librarian.

What will be most valuable to you is to engage with published research relevant to your enquiry; you should aim to read very recent research, where possible. Very often, this will require you to identify and read relevant journal articles. This can be time-consuming and you will need to be able to efficiently use the search facility of the journals database in the library that you are using. Many academic libraries provide written guidance and tutorials to support you in this process; again, seek further advice or support from a librarian if you are unsure about this. Depending on your focus, an efficient search using a journals database should yield quite a number of potential sources. Again, while you should aim to read widely, do ensure that you prioritise which articles you will read first and which you will read later, which you will read closely and which you will skim or scan; if you are teaching in sixth form, articles that refer to research undertaken in nursery settings are likely to be less relevant than those that refer to research undertaken in secondary schools, even if the focus matches yours. Although this process can be time-consuming, there are a number of significant benefits to engaging with research journal articles. For example, you may be able to find some very recent articles, which will increase their relevance to your enquiry. They also tend to have a very explicit focus on the 'how', rather than the 'why', which is exactly what you need when seeking to develop your own practice. Additionally, engaging with research journal articles provides you with the opportunity to be critical of the research undertaken, which can be very helpful in designing and undertaking your own research.

In addition to journal articles about single pieces of research, there is a great deal of value in engaging with published meta-analyses of research into teacher effectiveness. In simple terms, a meta-analysis is an analysis of a range of individual research projects that combines these to generate some overall findings. The main benefit of engaging with meta-analyses is that you can gain more of an overview of the key issues and the potential impact involved in one place. One easily accessible provider of meta-analyses is the Education Endowment Foundation (EEF), as referred to in Chapter 2. This body is a charity that funds evidence-based projects focusing on closing the attainment gap for children from low-income families. The projects, which are freely available on the EEF website, are grouped by type of approach, with a measure of impact, cost and evidence available. References are provided for the original research projects and meta-analyses upon which the measures are based, so can also lead you to further, relevant literature sources. Another potentially useful source is John Hattie's publication *Visible Learning: A Synthesis of Over 800 Meta-analyses Relating to Achievement* (2009), which brings together 15 years of research undertaken by himself and his team, providing what could be called a 'meta-meta-analysis'. The text provides references to the meta-analyses used, so could again be used to 'track back' to identify further, relevant literature sources. Over 100 additional meta-analyses have been included in his follow-up publication, *Visible Learning for Teachers: Maximizing Impact on Learning* (Hattie, 2012). As discussed in Chapter 1, it is worth noting that there are some potential limitations of meta-analyses: the more studies that are synthesised, the more the details and fine-grained insights can be lost, and the more the original methodologies used become obscured.

One way to consider your search for and reading of literature is as a branch diagram. When you read a source, whether it is overtly useful to you or not, it is always helpful to read the list of references at the end, as this can point you in the direction of other sources to seek out and read; in turn, these may point you in the direction of others. The process of reading to inform yourself before embarking upon the research is therefore a multi-stage process and, as mentioned at the start of this chapter, you will need to remain focused to ensure that you only travel down the relevant 'branches', rather than trying to read anything and everything. There is a fine balance to achieve between reading widely and reading in a focused manner.

CASE STUDY 4.1

Ralph, an undergraduate student teacher, is undertaking an action research enquiry for the dissertation module of his final year of primary teacher training. He has decided to focus on improving his questioning and to contextualise this within his teaching of religious education. After successfully agreeing on a focus and enquiry objectives with his dissertation supervisor, Ralph spends time engaging with literature before their next meeting.

At the tutorial, Ralph notes that he has read a great deal about the teaching of religious education, but that he has struggled to find much about teachers' questions in those texts. He comments that he has 'read lots about how important questioning is though' and is therefore feeling confident about undertaking the action research enquiry. Ralph's supervisor asks him to talk about what he has found out about effective questioning, and how that might inform his practice through the enquiry, and Ralph finds that he is unable to answer with any confidence.

This is an easy trap to fall into. Ralph has forgotten that the main emphasis for his reading should be on 'how' to do his focus as effectively as possible, by using literature to identify the key factors involved in effective questioning. Ideally, this literature should include as much research as possible, so that Ralph can find out about what has been effective for other teachers. Instead, he has become sidetracked by reading extensively about the value of questioning (the 'why', rather than the 'how'). Ralph was right to engage with some literature relating to the teaching of religious education, but it may have been more useful to wait until he had read about effective questioning, so that he could then make connections between the two, remembering that religious education is just a context to enable him to narrow down his enquiry: questioning is his main focus.

Ralph and his supervisor discuss returning to some of his previous literature sources to see whether they can help him begin to identify the key factors involved in effective questioning. They also discuss strategies for identifying new, more relevant sources for him to engage with. Ralph's supervisor suggests that he produces a mind map of the factors, following his further reading, to share at their next meeting.

HOW TO READ CRITICALLY

It is easy, particularly as a new or aspiring teacher, to assume that everything you read must be true as it has been written, and then published, by people with far more experience than you. However, if, as has been advised above, you read widely, you will begin to notice that some sources may present different views about the same issue. That does not necessarily mean that one is 'wrong'; both may be 'right', depending upon the context. What it does mean is that you need to develop your skills in reading critically, rather than taking everything at face value.

The first thing to consider when reading any source is whether it presents 'advice' (usually the opinion of the author) or whether it presents evidence and conclusions from research. It is very important to recognise the distinction between these two; while research will be evidence-based and therefore arguably more valuable, advice can still be useful to you but needs to be considered differently. Remember that your reading should focus on developing your knowledge and understanding of 'how' to develop your practice in the area of focus.

If the source is presenting advice, as many generic professional studies texts and subject-specific texts do, there are a number of questions you should aim to ask yourself:

Who is the author and what qualifies them to be giving advice? There is often a brief biography of the author, perhaps on the back cover or within the first few pages. Is the author a qualified teacher? Do they still teach now? How long have they been out of teaching? Are they still working with student teachers or qualified teachers? This will help you to consider whether their advice is based on their own experiences or whether it is merely their opinion, perhaps from their own reading or from observing others. If it is based on their experiences, are these relatable to your own experiences? For example, if their experiences were based in Key Stage 3 in large, inner-city schools and you are currently teaching Key Stage 1 in a small, rural school, this may lead you to consider how relevant this is to you; that does not mean that you should automatically discount it, but consider it alongside other reading and recognise that 'what worked' for the author may not be as effective for you in your very different context.

When was this published and where was this published? Although, depending on your focus, there may be some seminal pieces that should not be missed, more recent publications are generally seen to be more relevant and valuable to you. If there has been a significant shift in policy, you need to consider the date of publication in relation to the date of the policy change; for example, if your focus is the teaching of phonics, the date of publication of the *Independent Review of the Teaching of Early Reading* (Rose, 2006) and the subsequent policy adopted in response to this is highly significant; therefore, if reading texts published before this, you need to consider very carefully whether the 'advice' given is still relevant. The place of publication should also be carefully considered: if the piece was published in a different country from the one in which you are working, consider whether the educational systems are comparable and consider the relative importance of that with regard to your own selected focus.

Is the author drawing upon the work of others, whether that is also advice or whether it is research? If the author is drawing on the work of others, is this being done in a balanced and open manner, or is the author manipulating the work of others to fit their own agenda? It may only be possible to answer that by reading the original sources yourself.

How does the advice given compare with what you have read in other sources? Consider whether advice given agrees or disagrees with your previous reading. If the latter, consider the potential reasons for that, which may mean returning to some of the questions already posed above. Again, disagreement does not mean that you should discount the source and forget that you ever read it; just be aware that it contrasts with other sources, possibly for some very genuine reasons, and be open to the idea that your own experiences through undertaking the research may actually have more in common with this source than with those that seemed to be in agreement with each other.

If the source, such as a journal article, is presenting genuine research, you will need to consider the same questions as above, along with a number of others:

What was the nature and focus of the research and how closely does this align with your own focus? Consider whether the research is still relevant for you, if it is not closely aligned to your own focus. As discussed earlier in this chapter, you are unlikely to find many, if any, sources that address all aspects of your own enquiry. Remember that your focus, the aspect of practice that you wish to develop, is the most important factor. So, if your focus is providing pupils with effective written feedback and you are contextualising this within your teaching of geography to a class of Year 3 children, it is important that any pieces of published research that you engage with are also focused on effective written feedback (or feedback more generally); the subject and year group are less significant. Published research focused on providing effective written feedback in English with Year 6 children could still be very valuable to you, whereas a piece focused on questioning in geography with Year 3 children will not be because it will not add to your knowledge and understanding of 'how' to give effective written feedback.

How reliable is the research? In simple terms, 'reliability' in research relates to how 'repeatable' the results are; for research to be considered reliable, it would be possible for someone else to repeat it and obtain similar results. Anyone who has worked with children will know that there are multiple factors every single day that could make that impossible, no matter how hard the researchers try; it is impossible to replicate exactly the same conditions for all learners in any learning environment. However, the larger the sample size (the more children and/or schools involved), the more reliable it is likely to be. If the research was undertaken using an action research approach, as your own will be, it is more challenging to achieve reliability, as you are working with a small sample in a single context; as hard as you try to remain objective, another researcher would not teach in exactly the same way that you do. Therefore, you will also need to consider how important the issue of reliability, or lack of, really is, in relation to the other considerations.

How valid is the research? Validity relates to how effectively the research matches the intended objectives (and, in turn, the focus for the enquiry). There are two aspects to consider here: the process and the findings. Consider to what extent the process was valid and whether the process is even clearly explained. Consider whether the approach taken enabled the researchers to achieve the intended objectives or whether they actually researched something else entirely. Consider whether the findings are valid and whether they match the evidence presented. Consider whether you can see how the researcher arrived at the findings, based on the evidence gathered, or whether that is unclear. Consider whether the researcher has drawn upon more than one source/type of evidence to support their findings. This is known as triangulation and increases validity; this will be an important consideration in your own enquiry, as will be explored in Chapter 6. Consider whether the conclusions drawn are reasonable and do not 'overreach'. Teaching is a very complex business and it is easy to make assumptions about causation when there is correlation. For example, if the children in your class made significant progress in their understanding of a particular multiplication strategy while you were succeeding in improving your questioning skills, it would be easy to claim that the children's progress is due to the improvement in your questioning; in reality, the questioning is probably one of many factors involved in your teaching which contributed to this learning progress. When considering the value of a piece of research in relation to your own enquiry, validity is an important issue to consider.

Was the research conducted ethically? We will focus on the ethical issues that need to be considered when conducting educational research in the next chapter, but as well as considering this in relation to your own enquiry, you should also consider it as part of reading published research critically.

How does the research compare to your experience? Consider whether it aligns with what you already know about teaching and learning, either as a teacher or as a learner yourself. Your own judgement, based upon your own lived experience, is an important aspect of your reflection on the quality and value of what you read.

CRITICAL TASK 4.2

Hermione is undertaking the final placement of her PGCE, teaching geography in a secondary school. In her professional development training sessions, Hermione has heard others talking about developing children's metacognition and is interested in exploring this within her own practice through an action research enquiry. She has read literature about action research and has identified a focus and enquiry objectives. In order to start engaging with literature about her focus, Hermione starts by reading the *Metacognition and Self-regulated Learning: Summary of Recommendations* poster provided by the EEF (2020). This poster can be found in the Guidance Reports section on the EEF website.

Read through this poster yourself and then make some suggestions about what Hermione should consider reading next.

DEVELOPING A CRITICAL FRAMEWORK

Remember that, through reading widely and critically, you are seeking to develop your knowledge and understanding in relation to your focus. In addition, you should also aim to draw on your reading to synthesise a framework of criteria by which to judge the quality of your teaching and progress, and to judge the impact of your teaching on children's learning. You can refer to this framework to support your reflection at the end of each cycle, as well as your overall reflection at the end of the enquiry. We will explore how to present this framework as part of your literature review in Chapter 11.

RESPONSE TO CRITICAL TASK 4.1

As you have read through this chapter, you will have realised that there is a great deal for Anna to read before embarking upon her enquiry, but it would be sensible for her to start with some reading relating to the process of undertaking action research, as it is 'complex' (Cohen et al., 2018: 441) and quite different from the types of research that Anna might have encountered previously. It is therefore important that she has a clear understanding of the nature of action research before undertaking it. You might want to point her in the direction of this book.

RESPONSE TO CRITICAL TASK 4.2

In critical task 4.2, we told you that Hermione, a student teacher teaching geography in a secondary school, was interested in undertaking an action research enquiry to develop children's metacognition and that she had read the EEF's (2020) *Metacognition and Self-regulated Learning: Summary of Recommendations* poster. We asked you to consider what Hermione should consider reading next.

As explored in this chapter, it is important that Hermione reads critically, so she should be considering what the recommendations are based on, rather than just accepting them at face value. Not only would it be sensible to read the full guidance report that accompanies the poster, she should also engage with the evidence review, considering the research, and the interpretation of research findings, critically. The reference list at the end of the evidence review is likely to be very helpful in identifying other sources of literature for Hermione to read next.

SUMMARY FOR THIS CHAPTER

In this chapter, we have identified the importance of preparation for undertaking your enquiry through reading and have considered the scope of that reading. This stage of the process is very important, as without reading you will find it very difficult to develop your knowledge and understanding of 'how' to develop your practice, as well as finding it difficult to undertake the process of action research without understanding it. We have also considered how to read critically, rather than accepting what we read at face value, through comparing sources and raising questions about what we read. In the next chapter, we will explore ethical issues related to action research.

Do:

- undertake some reading before undertaking your action research project
- read literature that helps you to understand the process of undertaking action research, including the ethical considerations
- read literature that can inform your practice
- read widely
- read critically – do raise questions about what you read
- synthesise a critical framework for evaluating your teaching and its impact on learning.

Don't:

- believe everything you read . . .
- read so widely that you lose sight of your focus; you need to be selective
- get bogged down in reading policy or sources that do not help you to understand *how* to develop practice.

FURTHER READING

The following sources may also support you in engaging critically with literature and in further developing your knowledge and understanding of action research:

McNiff, J. and Whitehead, J. (2005) *Action Research for Teachers: A Practical Guide.* Abingdon: David Fulton Publishers.

As the title suggests, this text provides a practical guide for teachers undertaking action research in their classrooms and schools and includes some case studies to exemplify the process.

Wallace, M. and Poulson, L. (2004) 'Critical reading for self-critical writing', in L. Poulson and M. Wallace (eds), *Learning to Read Critically in Teaching and Learning.* London: Sage, pp. 3–36.

This chapter supports the reader to understand what it means to read 'critically' and provides some useful exercises to enable the reader to develop their skills. It also focuses on writing a literature review (so may also be relevant in relation to Chapter 11 of this book), but it is important to note that it does not specifically relate to education or to action research.

Williams, J. (2020) *How to Read and Understand Educational Research.* London: Sage.

For many new and aspiring teachers, engaging with literature about educational research can be a daunting prospect. This accessible text includes sections on assessing research, analysing research, and appreciating and understanding research.

Wyse, D. and Cowan, K. (2017) *The Good Writing Guide for Education Students.* 4th edn. London: Sage.

Chapter 1 of Wyse and Cowan's text provides a very accessible discussion regarding the importance of reading widely and how to approach this.

5

CONSIDERING
ETHICAL ISSUES

OBJECTIVES FOR THIS CHAPTER

- To explore the need to consider ethical issues in action research
- To consider the major ethical considerations in action research
- To explore some subtle ethical considerations in action research.

WHY ETHICS?

In this chapter, we will explore the importance of giving appropriate consideration to ethical issues when conducting action research, including those that are rather subtle and require a careful approach. We begin by considering the need for ethical frameworks within research and within action research in particular.

Within all research, ethical frameworks are designed to provide protection for the participants, to ensure that they come to no harm and are in no way disadvantaged as a result of taking part in the research. In any research context, researchers take appropriate steps to ensure that their project does not have any negative impacts on the participants, particularly if these are in any way deemed to be vulnerable: children and young people are always deemed to be vulnerable in relation to research. The British Educational Research Association provides ethical guidelines, which are updated regularly, for conducting educational research with children and young people and these form essential reading for anyone planning on undertaking any kind of research project within education, as they explore both the principles and practice of undertaking an ethically sound project (BERA, 2018).

It is possible for student teachers undertaking action research to feel that their projects present little ethical concern, and this can lead to insufficient consideration being given to ethical issues. We have already established the nature of education action research as a process in which a new or aspiring teacher seeks to develop and enhance their practice through gathering and analysing evidence about the impact of their teaching on children's learning. The emphasis is on developing best practice through using readily available evidence about the children's learning to inform evaluation and plan for improvement. As a result, it would be easy for student teachers undertaking action research projects to see ethics as of limited significance within this kind of study, as the focus is unlikely to be ethically contentious and the student teacher is just 'doing what teachers do', evaluating practice on the basis of the children's learning, in a formal or structured manner. Further, some might argue that teachers take responsibility for children and young people's welfare through acting *in loco parentis* on a daily basis and so already carry a significant ethical duty of care to act in the best interests of their pupils. However, there are several key reasons why, even in education action research, which appears, on the surface, to be relatively uncontentious, ethical issues need to be addressed through careful consideration and appropriate action and, as Brooks et al. (2014: 59) argue, 'it is important to think carefully about the ethical implications of research from the very earliest stages'.

RESEARCH WITH VULNERABLE GROUPS

Ethical issues are important within education action research because of the innate vulnerability of children and young people (Silverman, 2017). Children are in the care of the teacher and the school, and anyone who enters into a piece of research using these vulnerable subjects as participants must ensure that they have weighed carefully the impact of their project, to ensure that it carries no risk of harm, including no risk of unintended detrimental impact on the pupils' learning or progress. Clearly, no teacher planning an action research project would deliberately set out to cause harm to the learners, but if the planned approach could have any potential negative impact on the children's progress then it should be reconsidered. As such, it is important that all action research projects are discussed with other professionals, as a safeguard against any possible negative impacts on children or young people.

THE ROLE OF THE RESEARCHER AS A TEACHER

There is an unavoidable imbalance of power in the relationships between children and teachers, in relation to both teaching and the research project. The duality of the student teacher's role, as both educator and researcher, means that they need to develop an awareness of this imbalance and take proactive steps to ensure that they do not, in any way, abuse their position of trust. They should, for example, ensure that they do not expect children to take part in unusual activities that have been designed purely for the purpose of the research project, either in the teaching or when gathering evidence.

OPENNESS AND RESPECT FOR ALL PARTIES

It is tempting to think that, as action research is just about developing good practice, it is not necessary for the children or young people involved to be aware of the research. Indeed, some student teachers might worry that alerting the children to the research might lead to unnatural responses from the children and so argue that it would be best if they remained unaware of it. However, to undertake 'covert' research in this way would suggest a lack of respect for the pupils or even a lack of trust in their ability to understand and appreciate the nature and purpose of the action research process. If they are central to the process (and with action research they are) then it is appropriate to treat them with respect and be open about the nature and purpose of your research. Similarly, you will want to be open with colleagues and parents about why you are undertaking your action research and what it involves, as we will explore later in this chapter.

'OWNERSHIP' OF EVIDENCE

In education action research, much of the evidence gathered for the study will relate to the children's learning, such as examples of their written work, their drawings or even their spoken words. Again, it is possible to argue that, since this evidence is only of the kind that the aspiring teacher has access to every day, it would be ethically acceptable, for the purpose of the study, to take copies of their work or make note of their words without requesting the permission from the child or young person, but this approach would demonstrate a lack of respect for the original 'owner' of the evidence. In using a child's writing, drawings or spoken words in our research, we should acknowledge that this evidence is not ours and that we are making use of the intellectual property of someone else for our own ends, even if those ends are very worthy and laudable.

RESPECT FOR KNOWLEDGE

BERA (2018) identifies that all education research should value and respect knowledge and that all researchers should aim to conduct high quality research; this applies just as much to action research as any other kind, and such projects undertaken by new and aspiring teachers should be approached seriously, with appropriate rigour, and with a commitment to honest and truthful reporting of the research process and findings. In particular, student teachers undertaking education action research should avoid being unnecessarily self-congratulatory in their approach, keeping in mind that the purpose of the project is not to prove what a brilliant teacher they are but how much they have learnt about their own practice as a teacher.

THE PRINCIPLE OF CAUSING NO HARM OR DISADVANTAGE

Action research, in the way in which we have described it in this book, appears to be a relatively benign process, in which a good teacher seeks to become a better teacher through the analysis of evidence related to their practice. However, even in action research, it is important to be aware of the central principle of ethical research: that it should cause no harm or disadvantage to the participants. In fact, it is also important that your action research should not unfairly advantage one pupil or group of pupils over others in your class. No teacher would deliberately set out to cause harm through their research, or to offer some children preferential treatment over others, but without giving these issues careful consideration, it may be that some unintended consequences of our actions do lead to these outcomes.

MAJOR ETHICAL CONSIDERATIONS IN ACTION RESEARCH

There are several well-established practices to be considered when planning an action research project, all of which follow on from the principles outlined above.

GATEKEEPERS

In education action research, the term 'gatekeepers' refers to the people who should give permission for a research project to be undertaken. As noted by Kay (2019: 37), 'gatekeepers exist in various strata within a research project [and] serve an important role in testing the applications of the principles of beneficence and non-maleficence within the proposed research'. Student teachers are likely to go through a process, within their university or college, to demonstrate that they have given sufficient consideration to how they will undertake their research in a way that does not cause any ethical concerns. Once on placement, key staff within the school, college or other education setting should be informed about the study and asked for their permission to proceed with the project. In most cases, this will include the headteacher or principal or another senior member of staff, as well as other key members of staff who work with the children or young people involved.

It is important to go through these gatekeepers for three reasons. Firstly, it provides a check that the principle of causing no harm is being given appropriate consideration, as the gatekeepers will only agree to the study if they are content that it poses no threat to the welfare or learning of the children or young people. They will be able to refer you to relevant school policies, such as those related to taking photographs or the use of video cameras. Secondly, the senior team will be able to advise how your study fits with any school improvement priorities and may suggest some ways in which it might be adjusted to be more helpful to the school's development. Thirdly, they are likely to be able to help and suggest ways to improve the study, through recommending relevant resources or arranging for you to meet with local teachers who are leaders in the area of your enquiry.

INFORMED CONSENT AND THE RIGHT TO WITHDRAW

As identified earlier, it is important to be open with all parties about your action research, to give them information about what you plan to do and what you hope to achieve by doing so, and to give them the opportunity to choose whether to take part or not. It is worth being clear at this point as to what you are requesting consent for or, more precisely, what you are not requesting consent for. You are not requesting permission to *teach* the children or young people, as that is your job as a teacher: you are seeking consent to gather evidence in relation to their learning.

You should seek informed consent from parental guardians *and* the children or young people in your class; how you do this will clearly be dependent on the age of the children and the nature of the study and we will explore this further in Chapter 7.

If you intend to disseminate the results of your study through a conference or publication, or if you think there is a chance you may wish to do so at some stage in the future, it is a good idea to seek full informed consent in the early stages of your project.

CONFIDENTIALITY AND ANONYMITY

It is the responsibility of the researcher to keep personal or sensitive details of the study confidential throughout the process. During the study, you should not discuss specific details with teachers outside your own school, and take care, when speaking to friends or using social media, not to inadvertently reveal any information about the children or the study. When writing the account of the research as a report or assignment, as we will discuss further in Part 3, you should ensure that none of the participants are identifiable through your account.

DATA MANAGEMENT

It is your responsibility to ensure that all your data is kept securely for the duration of the project. It is normally considered good practice to delete or destroy sensitive evidence, such as audio-recordings, once the project is completed. A word of caution, here: if you are writing up your project as part of any academic award, do not delete your evidence until you are sure you have passed the module. If you plan to publish work or to use the data you have gathered as part of a longer-term project, you may want to retain secondary data, such as transcripts of audio-recordings, for longer. The important principle here is that you should be clear with your participants from the outset about how you will store the data in both the short and longer term.

CRITICAL TASK 5.1

Ashraf is a student teacher undertaking a BA (QTS) programme. He is keen to improve his written feedback in English lessons to help children make good progress with their writing. He plans to start his enquiry by providing minimal feedback and develop this over time to provide more feedback of a more detailed nature. What advice would you give to Ashraf about his plans to ensure that they become more ethical?

SUBTLE ETHICAL CONSIDERATIONS IN ACTION RESEARCH

Thomas (2017: 36) makes this valuable point that should guide all educational research:

> It is important to remember that ethics is much more than a practical matter – it is about the conduct of your work: it is about how you think about inquiry, how you think about this research project: it is about your respect for others.

This applies particularly to action research, which brings some subtle ethical consider-ations that are not necessarily present in other forms of research, and new and aspiring teachers should be aware of them and take positive steps to ensure that they avoid any difficulties.

BEST PRACTICE AT ALL TIMES

A key principle of action research is that the teacher must give of their best to all of the learners at all times, in accordance with Article 3 of the United Nations Convention on the Rights of the Child, which states that 'the best interests of the child must be a top priority in all decisions and actions that affect children'. There is, perhaps, a temptation, which must be resisted, to begin an action research project by teaching slightly below your best, in order to demonstrate how your practice improves over the time of the enquiry. Just to be clear, this would be unethical! Not only that, but you would be depriving your-self of the opportunity to genuinely improve your practice over time. From day one of the enquiry, the teacher must plan and teach to the best of their ability. As we explored in Chapter 4, it will be valuable to inform your understanding of good practice through appropriate engagement with relevant literature, so that you can be confident that your approach is informed by recent and relevant research about high-impact teaching.

NO EXPERIMENTS

On a similar theme, it is important to remember that action research is not about 'trying out' or 'comparing' different teaching approaches to see which is most effective. To do so would inevitably involve the researcher in planning and teaching some lessons that were less than their best or, even worse, using different teaching approaches with different groups of children to 'see which is best'.

USE OF A 'FOCUS GROUP'

To make the process of gathering detailed evidence more manageable, it is often useful to identify a 'focus group' of children or young people. This might be a group of five or six individuals about whom the researcher gathers a range of detailed evidence in order to gain meaningful insights into their learning over time. From an ethical point of view, the term 'focus group' is somewhat unhelpful, as it gives the impression that the research should 'focus' on that group; as we have already established that no group or individual within the class should be either advantaged or disadvantaged as a result of the action research, this would clearly be unethical. So, while it is often useful to identify a number of children about whom the researcher gathers more detailed evidence, a focus group should not be treated differently from any other group within the class. There is a subtle tension here, which will need to be managed throughout the study.

CRITICAL TASK 5.2

The use of a focus group is much more problematic for some action research projects than for others. Have a look at the projects identified in Table 5.1 and consider whether you would want to use a focus group for this project.

Table 5.1 Ethical tensions in use of a focus group

Enquiry focus	Would you use a focus group?
Improving my written feedback in English to support progress in writing	
Improving my use of questioning to enhance young people's learning in science	
Improving the way I embed children's self-assessment to impact positively on their progress in mathematics	

EVIDENCE

We will consider how to gather appropriate evidence in Chapters 6 and 8, but it is worth noting here that, throughout the study, the researcher should ensure that any evidence they gather is appropriate and should consider any ethical implications. For example, in some action research projects, it may be valuable to take photographs of the children at work; in this case, care must be taken to ensure compliance with any school policies on this issue and the anonymity of children must be protected throughout.

In general it is best to avoid interviews, as children may feel coerced to say what they think you want to hear or feel uncomfortable about expressing their honest opinions. We may try to convince ourselves that we have an open, trusting and reciprocal relationship with the children or young people we work with; however, there will always exist a power imbalance, which means that children are unlikely to be entirely honest in their responses in an interview. Consequently, not only have the children been put in an uncomfortable position, but the evidence does not provide a 'truthful' insight into the teaching and learning process.

SHARE YOUR FINDINGS WITH THE SCHOOL COMMUNITY

Towards the end of the project, it is good practice to agree with the school on how you might share your findings with key members of staff, parents and children. This is an important step in being open about the evidence that you have gathered and what you have learnt from the process.

STAY FOCUSED ON YOUR OWN PRACTICE

Finally, a reminder that any evidence that you gather should focus on your own practice and not that of others. You should never seek feedback from children or young people about another teacher or colleague and you should never set out to demonstrate that you are a better teacher than anyone else!

CRITICAL TASK 5.3

Ashraf plans to use a focus group to help gather some deep insights into the impact of his marking on learners' progress. He plans to take copies of work from this group and to sit

(Continued)

---

with them each day while they read his comments so that he can observe their responses. He intends to interview this group during lunchtimes to ask them about the feedback he has provided and how it might be improved. What advice would you give to Ashraf about the ethical implications of his approach and how it might be improved?

RESPONSE TO CRITICAL TASK 5.1

Ashraf has chosen a suitable focus for his study, as he knows that providing high quality feedback on children's learning is an important part of the work of a highly effective teacher, and he is responding to feedback from his previous placement report that this is an area of his practice that he should seek to develop. He has also got the idea that action research is about improving practice over time; however, he has forgotten that he should be doing his best at all times, so he needs to start with his best marking right from the start of the process, and use evidence about the children's learning to evaluate the impact it has on their progress and, as a result, get better at using his marking to have a positive impact on the learners' progress. As a word of advice for Ashraf, we might recommend that he focuses on how he engages the young people with his marking, not just on the quality of the marking itself: fantastic marking will have little impact unless the learners engage with it, and, over time, through evaluation, Ashraf might become better at involving the children in the process. He might also wish to return to his reading about good practice in this area, to further inform the improvement of his teaching and the outcomes for the learners.

RESPONSE TO CRITICAL TASK 5.2

The use of a focus group is much more problematic for some action research projects than for others. In this critical task, we asked you to look at the enquiry foci identified in Table 5.1 and consider whether you would want to use a focus group for this project. We offer our own thoughts in Table 5.2.

Table 5.2 Ethical tensions in use of a focus group (revisited)

Enquiry focus	Would you use a focus group?
Improving my written feedback in English to support progress in writing	Yes. It would be important to mark all books with similar care and attention to detail, but absolutely fine to have a focus group whose progress is tracked more closely. Take care not to give this group any more attention than other learners in lessons or when observing children's responses to feedback.

Enquiry focus	Would you use a focus group?
Improving my use of questioning to enhance young people's learning in science	No. Questions asked by teachers are normally open to the whole class and it would distort your approach to teaching if you focused on just a small number of learners within the class.
Improving the way I embed children's self-assessment to impact positively on their progress in mathematics	Yes and no. It would be a good idea to have a focus group of children whose work is analysed in detail after lessons. Within lessons, it would be important not to focus on this group but to gather other evidence about the way in which you engage children in self-assessment and the ways in which they respond to this.

RESPONSE TO CRITICAL TASK 5.3

Ashraf has the right idea, that observing how the learners engage with his marking is likely to be revealing and may help him improve his approach to engaging all learners with his written feedback. However, as his plans stand, he runs the risk of focusing too much on his focus group. The point of the focus group is to allow Ashraf to see the detail of the impact of his developing practice over time, by focusing on a small sample within the class, but this should not stop him from gathering evidence from the whole class. By sitting with his focus group every day, to the exclusion of others, it looks like they are getting more of his attention than other learners. Keeping the group in at lunchtime to interview reinforces the idea that this group is in some way 'special' to Ashraf, although the young people in the group might argue that being kept in at lunchtime is a definite disadvantage. Finally, Ashraf is inadvertently putting this group under unnecessary pressure by asking for their opinions on his marking and, what is more, this is unlikely to yield evidence with strong validity.

SUMMARY FOR THIS CHAPTER

In this chapter, we have considered some of the key ethical issues that the action researcher needs to take into account when planning a project, and some of the more subtle issues that might arise. In reality, these can only ever be guidelines and the ethical researcher will be responsive as well as proactive in managing the complex issues involved in an action research enquiry. Keep in mind the principles of being open with participants and colleagues, maintaining confidentiality outside the context, doing your best teaching at all times and ensuring there is no harm to the children or young people and you won't go too far wrong. In the next chapter, we will consider how to plan to gather useful data.

Do:

- refer to the British Educational Research Association for ethical guidelines
- seek support from ethical gatekeepers
- seek informed consent from parents and children
- maintain confidentiality
- ensure you offer your best teaching to all children at all times
- treat all children equitably
- gather good quality and meaningful evidence
- plan to share your findings with your school.

Don't:

- be lazy about ethics
- plan 'experiments' or 'tests' that might advantage or disadvantage some children
- talk about the details of your research outside the school or setting context.

FURTHER READING

The following sources may also support you in reflecting on good ethical practice:

Miller, T. and Bell, L. (2012) 'Consenting to what? Issues of access, gate-keeping and "informed" consent', in T. Miller, B. Birch, M. Mauthner and J. Jessop (eds), *Ethics in Qualitative Research*. 2nd edn. London: Sage, pp. 61–75.

This very helpful chapter tackles issues related to the ongoing nature of ethical concerns throughout the duration of an enquiry.

The Research Ethics Guidebook: A Guide for Social Scientists:
www.ethicsguidebook.ac.uk

This website is a great resource providing practical and current advice about good ethical practice in social science research.

United Nations Convention on the Rights of the Child (UNCRC):
www.unicef.org.uk/UNICEFs-Work/UN-Convention

This is an international statement on the rights of children and should underpin all work for those who work with children and young people.

6

PLANNING TO GATHER DATA

OBJECTIVES FOR THIS CHAPTER

- To consider the benefits of qualitative data
- To explore the range of data sources which could provide valuable information
- To consider how best to plan to 'capture' data
- To explore the concepts of reliability, validity, triangulation.

QUALITATIVE DATA

In this chapter, we will explore the kind of data that will be beneficial to new and aspiring teachers when exploring their practice through action research. We will also grapple with some technical terms and issues in relation to research.

It is worth mentioning here that some authors (for example, Holliday, 2016) draw a technical distinction between data and evidence which it is worth being aware of: 'data' refers to all the raw information that a researcher gathers and 'evidence' refers to those particular aspects of the data that the researcher chooses to present in their analysis and findings. In this book, we often use the terms interchangeably because, in action research, data very quickly becomes evidence, because of the 'real-time' nature of the enquiry process.

Quantitative data is used to quantify phenomena through the use of numbers whereas qualitative data is used to describe phenomena through non-numerical means, such as through the 'capture' of words or pictures. Both can be used to provide an insight into the nature of the real, complex world of teaching and learning within schools and other settings and both have their strengths and limitations. However, within small-scale action research, the value of quantitative data is limited, whereas the richness of qualitative data is valuable in providing meaningful insights into a complex process, which can be examined in detail.

One of the main reasons that quantitative data tends not to be useful in action research relates to the limitations of statistical analysis with small samples. Research undertaken in just one setting or with one group of learners is unlikely to generate enough quantitative data to enable meaningful analysis. Similarly, action research projects undertaken by new and aspiring teachers tend to be run over short timescales in which quantitative data is unlikely to provide meaningful insights about learners' progress.

There may be some situations where gathering some quantitative data, alongside the qualitative data, might be helpful. For example, if you are focusing on improving your questioning, your reading has probably helped you to identify that teachers can sometimes ask too many questions. You might therefore want to gather data in relation to how many questions you planned to ask and how many you actually ask in a lesson. This should complement your collection of qualitative data, however, rather than replacing it. Simply knowing that you ask lots of questions is not going to help you focus on the quality of those questions, or on their impact on children's learning.

Some new or aspiring teachers may feel uncomfortable with the emphasis on qualitative data, particularly if they have previously worked or studied in the natural or physical sciences. They may feel that qualitative data is 'soft', open to interpretation and difficult to analyse. They may find themselves tempted to convert qualitative data into quantitative data through, for example, the use of scales and this temptation should be resisted as, by doing so, the richness of the original data is lost and the validity of the quantitative interpretation is questionable, as it does not represent real or raw data, but a manipulated version of it.

CRITICAL TASK 6.1

Remember Jane, the School Direct PGCE primary student teacher who wants to improve the way she meets individual needs by differentiating recording of learning in science? She has decided on her objectives, which are:

- to understand how the children engage with recording their science learning
- to analyse the impact of the children's recording on their science learning
- to evaluate my approach to engaging children in meaningful recording of their science learning.

She needs to decide the data that she should gather that would help her to understand how effective her practice is and how she can improve it. What kind of data should she plan to gather?

SOME SOURCES OF POTENTIALLY RICH QUALITATIVE DATA

Data is only rich if it is directly relevant to your focus and addresses your enquiry objectives and that is why it is important to be really clear about your focus, the kinds of data that will help provide some valuable insights in relation to the focus, what you will look for in that data and, really importantly, to plan, in advance, how to capture really good data. Here are some sources of evidence that are likely to be rich and valuable.

COPIES OF CHILDREN'S OR YOUNG PEOPLE'S WRITTEN OR PICTORIAL WORK

Remember that the best evidence is that which helps you to understand the impact of your teaching on the progress of the learners, so the independent recording of their learning can be a very revealing and rich source of data. The extent to which the learners' recording is independent is an important consideration, as anything that is too heavily 'guided' – 'copying off the board' being one of the worst examples – or too open to plagiarism, such as copy and pasting from the internet, will not provide real insights into genuine learning. Work that provides genuine opportunities for the children or young people to demonstrate what they know or understand will provide insights into their learning, so it will be important to know what you are going to 'look for' in their work. This will normally require looking at some specific details of the work, so you should avoid being distracted by 'surface' features such as how much they have written or presentational features such as neatness.

OBSERVATIONS OF LEARNERS

It is often beneficial for teachers to take a step back for a moment during a lesson, to observe what is going on and how the learners are engaging with the task at hand. This may involve a broad sweep of looking across the whole class or observing one individual or a small group, to see how they are interacting with each other and the learning process. It is important to be clear about what you are looking for when observing and to build the opportunities for doing so into your lesson plans.

Wragg (2012: 51) notes that 'we often interpret events as we wish to see them, not as they are'. When observing children or young people at work, try to note only what you see and hear and avoid making statements or comments about the meaning of your observations; save that for later when you have time to be analytical about the meaning of the children's or young people's actions or behaviours.

WORDS CHILDREN SAY

Some of the most revealing of all evidence about children's or young people's learning are the things that they say, as these provide a glimpse of what is going on inside their heads. However, as with their written or pictorial work, consideration must be given to how independent the words are and how well they reflect the pupils' actual thoughts and how much they may be influenced by those around them, including, most significantly, you the teacher; children are likely to modify what they say depending on the level of approval they anticipate their words may receive.

One of the challenges with using children's spoken words as evidence is the transient nature of the data, which means that it is hard to 'capture'. A child may say something brilliantly relevant to your enquiry, revealing something significant about their learning, but a few moments later you just can't remember what it was. Teaching involves many interactions with learners every hour and it is impossible to remember them all. So it is important to plan ahead so that you have a clear idea of how you will avoid important insights slipping through your fingers. This can be achieved through audio-recording, video-recording or taking notes, and each of these has its own benefits, challenges and ethical considerations. With the advent of smartphones and other modern gadgetry, audio-recording is easier than ever, and it can be a useful way of ensuring that you have a reliable record of the words that have been uttered in your lesson. However, the ethical implications of electronically 'capturing' a part of someone else's life have not changed, so the ethical safeguards of consent and confidentiality should be observed, as explored in the previous chapter.

There are three main practical challenges with audio-recording. The first relates to the quality of the recording, which is dependent not just on the technology, but also on the teaching context in which the recording is made: lots of background noise can render a recording almost useless. The second practical issue to be considered is the impact that the act of recording may have on the natural behaviour of the participants, as they may 'play up' for the camera or become subdued and reluctant to contribute. The final practical issue is finding the time for listening to the recordings and transcribing them into written records while managing the demands of teaching, planning and marking. The good news is that it is not normally necessary to transcribe all the audio-recordings that you have made, and it is usually beneficial to identify some short sections that are noteworthy in some way and to make short transcripts of these sections: we call these 'transcriptlets' and we will discuss them further in Part 3.

The least technological way of capturing evidence of words learners say is by making notes and this approach also has some advantages and challenges to be considered in advance. The challenges are, perhaps, obvious: it is almost impossible to write down every word that children or young people say, so it should be accepted that the record will be an approximation of what was said rather than a word-for-word account. It is also difficult to record words spoken within a lesson while also teaching that same lesson, so it will be important to plan for when this might be possible and draw on support from other colleagues in the process of creating a record of interactions. Making notes of conversations has some advantages over using an audio-recorder: the researcher can note just the interesting comments and do so in a 'naturalistic' way, without influencing (too much) the normal behaviour of the participants.

The words that learners utter are always open to interpretation (as is all data) so care must be taken to try to record these as accurately as possible, while always ensuring that the teaching and learning are prioritised over the gathering of data.

THIRD-PARTY FEEDBACK ON YOUR TEACHING

It is a good idea to ask for feedback on your teaching from a more experienced teacher. Observations of teaching are common for new teachers, particularly for those still in training and those who are newly qualified, and they offer a good opportunity to receive valuable and objective insights into your teaching and its impact. These can be wide-ranging, providing commentary on many aspects of a lesson or practice, so it is beneficial for the new teacher undertaking an action research project to be explicit with their mentor about the specific focus on which they would value feedback: the more specific you can be, the more focused your colleague can be in providing you with insights related to your practice.

DISCUSSIONS WITH A MENTOR

In addition to mentors being able to provide third-party feedback on your teaching, engaging in, and keeping a record of, discussions with a mentor about your chosen focus can also be a useful source of data. Such discussions might help you to make sense of your reading, through considering how it might apply to your particular context. Your mentor might also share their own thoughts about effective practice in the selected aspect of teaching. Finally, the mentor may also act as a 'critical friend', who Foulger (2010: 140) suggests can 'provide alternative perspectives, support and protection from bias', as you gather and seek to interpret the evidence; the notion of a critical friend will be discussed further in Chapter 9.

LESSON OR DAILY EVALUATIONS

New and aspiring teachers often overlook a valuable source of evidence that they can create themselves as part of their usual reflective practice: their lesson or daily evaluations. These can provide a useful record of your reflections on your teaching, written on the day of the lesson(s), with your honest thoughts about how well you were achieving the targets set for yourself in relation to your focus and how this was impacting on the learning.

There is an obvious and common objection to the use of personal evaluation as a kind of data, as it is both created by and used by the same researcher as part of their study and therefore lacks objectivity. However, when we remind ourselves that, for new and aspiring teachers, the purpose of action research is not to add to the body of knowledge about teaching and learning but to develop their individual practice, the personal, on-the-spot evaluations of that teacher can be seen as a very valuable source of evidence. As we will discuss below, a teacher should still aim to approach this evidence with objectivity, through comparing it to other data gathered from the same learning episodes.

SOME SOURCES OF QUALITATIVE DATA THAT MAY BE LESS RICH

Some sources of data may not yield as much useful evidence as hoped.

PHOTOGRAPHS

Photographs are normally limited as a source of evidence. They can provide evidence of something that a child has done but tend not to reveal very much about what a child has learnt. That is not to say that photographs cannot be a valuable source of data, but that careful planning is required so that the pictures provide meaningful insights into learning rather than just evidence of activity.

THIRD-PARTY OBSERVATION OF CHILDREN

It is often a good idea to ask another adult in the classroom to support you in the process of gathering data, but it is important to be very clear with your colleagues about what your evidence should focus on. Comments such as 'Matthew worked very hard' or 'Gemma was being a bit silly today' will not provide you with meaningful insights into Matthew's and Gemma's learning, but, with careful planning, you may be able to ensure that your colleagues understand what kind of details will be useful to you. It may be helpful to give some thought to the paperwork that you ask to be filled in, perhaps with the key learning objectives noted, and you might ask your colleagues to jot down things that the children say in relation to these.

INTERVIEWS WITH CHILDREN OR YOUNG PEOPLE

Interviews are not recommended within action research for two interrelated reasons: one is an ethical objection related to the imbalance of power between the researcher and the participant as a result of their parallel relationship as teacher and learner (which we will consider further in Chapter 7), and the other is a methodological objection. The main problem with teachers interviewing their own pupils about the quality and impact of their teaching is that, as Koshy (2010) notes, they are only likely to be told what they want to hear, as it is very difficult for a child or young person to be honest with teachers about these issues. However, it is possible for teachers to discuss their pupils' learning with them through the use of 'learning conferences', which we will discuss further in Chapter 7.

PLANNING TO 'CAPTURE' GOOD EVIDENCE

It is helpful to plan, in advance, how you will capture good evidence, as part of the busy schedule of teaching: plan when you will observe learners, be proactive about requesting feedback on your teaching, plan which lessons you might evaluate in detail and which pieces of work will be valuable to scan or photograph.

THE USE OF A 'FOCUS GROUP'

In addition to gathering data about your teaching and its impact on the class as a whole, it is also sometimes useful (depending on your enquiry focus) to gather more focused information about the learning of a smaller sample of the whole group, to provide a detailed picture of their learning over time.

However, the term 'focus group' is, in some ways, misleading and unhelpful. As we discuss further in Chapters 5 and 7, it is important to treat all children and young people equitably, so a focus group should only be a focus in relation to the collection of data, not in terms of your time or attention within your teaching. It is also important not to ignore interesting insights that occur with children's learning outside the focus group, and the focus group can change and develop over time, depending on the nature of your enquiry.

When intending to capture observation data of any kind, including making notes of children's words, it is useful to develop a plan in relation to how this data will 'look' and to think about ways in which to make the process of capturing the information as easy for yourself as possible. It may be helpful to design a pro forma or table to make it easier or quicker to note the key observations or words.

In addition to being proactive about the process, you should also be opportunistic and take unanticipated opportunities as they arise to gather further insights into the learning of the children or young people. These 'critical incidents' can occur outside formal lessons, such as in the playground or when on school trips, or in discussion with colleagues or parents. Any moment that gives you something to think about in relation to your focus is worth noting.

CRITICAL TASK 6.2

In Critical task 6.1, we asked you to consider the types of data that might be useful to Jane, who wants to improve the way she meets individual needs by differentiating recording of learning in science. Jane has decided to use a focus group for her enquiry. Having read the advice above, Jane thinks it would be a good idea for her to design a pro forma or table to help her keep a record of her observations. Can you help Jane by designing a pro forma or table for her to use?

SOME TECHNICAL TERMS: RELIABILITY, VALIDITY AND TRIANGULATION

There are a few technical terms that are worth clarifying at this stage. 'Reliability' refers to the extent to which a study's findings could be repeatable or reproducible and this normally relates to the size of the sample. In education research, this normally means that the larger the number of children or schools involved in a study, the greater the degree of reliability. However, just because a particular study is large in scale does not guarantee that its findings are trustworthy or meaningful, and this is where validity comes in. 'Validity' refers to the extent to which a study has good alignment between what it was trying to find out (its objectives), the appropriateness of the data gathered in relation to the objectives, the quality of the analysis of the evidence and, as a result of all that, how convincing the reported findings are. One way to increase the validity of a study is for the researcher to use triangulation, in which more than one kind of data (but not necessarily three kinds), or data from more than one source (but not necessarily three sources), are utilised in a rigorous way to build a coherent picture of the situation being researched, with a sound and detailed exploration of the complexities.

It is unlikely that your own action research enquiry will have high reliability, as you will be undertaking a small-scale study in just one educational setting, involving a small number of children or young people. This is not a problem: it is in the nature of the kind of enquiry you are embarking upon. However, it is important that you should aim to ensure that your study has high validity through effective use of a triangulated approach to both the gathering and analysis of data.

CRITICAL TASK 6.3

Sophie is a School Direct PGCE student, about to embark on a placement in a Key Stage 1 class. She is keen to focus on developing her use of resources to support and enhance learning with this age group and has decided to contextualise her enquiry in mathematics. Sophie feels that photographs will be one valuable source of evidence for her, as these can show how children have made use of the resources in their learning, but she understands that there are limitations to the use of photographs. She also recognises the importance of triangulation to increase the validity of her enquiry.

What other sources of data might Sophie collect, alongside the photographs?

RESPONSE TO CRITICAL TASK 6.1

We asked you to suggest the kinds of data that Jane should gather. The key thing is that she should gather evidence that relates directly to her objectives:

- to understand how the children engage with recording their science learning:
  - o data: observation of the children at work, notes of words spoken by the children, the children's work
- to analyse the impact of the children's recording on their science learning:
  - o data: the children's work, assessments, notes of words spoken by the children, assessment information
- to evaluate my approach to engaging children in meaningful recording of their science learning:
  - o data: lesson or daily evaluations, third-party feedback.

While it is important for Jane to ensure that she gathers some evidence in relation to each objective, these are, of course, very interrelated.

RESPONSE TO CRITICAL TASK 6.2

In Critical task 6.2, we asked you to design a pro forma or table for Jane to use, to make it easier for her keep a record of her observations. As Jane has decided to use a focus group, it would be helpful if the pro forma or table had a row for each of the children in the focus group. A 'spare' row or two would also be helpful in case Jane notes anything particularly significant in relation to other children in the class, which would not already be captured in her lesson evaluation or assessment records. Jane may then need columns to record things such as:

- which recording method each child in the focus group used
- whether the recording method was chosen by the child or directed by Jane
- whether the child needed any support to record their learning
- whether the child met the intended learning outcome for the lesson
- whether the recording task reinforced the learning
- whether the record of learning matches Jane's own assessment of what the child knows, understands and can do.

As Jane will be adapting her practice in relation to her focus in each cycle, seeking to improve it as much as possible, it may be that her pro forma or table needs to alter slightly for each cycle, in order to ensure that it supports her in collecting useful data.

RESPONSE TO CRITICAL TASK 6.3

Sophie is undertaking an action research enquiry, focusing on developing her use of resources to support and enhance learning. In this task, we asked you to consider what other forms of data Sophie might plan to collect, alongside photographs, in order to triangulate her evidence.

It is important to remember that photographs capture a single moment in time and are usually a record of action, rather than learning. In this enquiry, a photograph of resources after a child has used them to solve a calculation might be useful. For example, a photograph of seven green cubes and five red cubes, alongside a completed addition number sentence on a mini whiteboard, might be helpful in showing how the child used the resources. However, Sophie is focusing on her own use of the resources, not just the children's use of the resources, so she may have annotated her lesson plan to show any changes that she made to the original plan and this annotated lesson plan may therefore be a useful source of evidence. Her evaluation will also provide useful evidence of how effectively she feels she used the resources. Her assessment records will provide evidence of whether or not children met the intended learning outcome for the lesson. Observation notes will provide useful evidence in relation to how the children engaged with the resources provided. In the example above, the child may have solved the addition number sentence '7 + 5' mentally and put the cubes out afterwards, having seen that other children had used them. On its own, the photograph might suggest the child used the cubes to find the answer, but when combined with the observation notes that might not have been the case.

Sophie should also consider her use of photographs carefully from an ethical point of view, ensuring that anonymity is maintained and that all parties consent to photographs being taken and used in this way, as discussed in the previous chapter. In the example above, the child would not need to be in the photograph at all, but this might not be the case in all situations.

SUMMARY FOR THIS CHAPTER

In this chapter, we have considered the value of gathering rich qualitative data and the benefits of planning ahead to facilitate this. We have identified some sources of data as being potentially rich in providing insights into learning, such as copies of written work, observation of learners at work and the words that they say and, importantly, your own evaluation notes; we have also noted some of the potential limitations of some approaches to gathering evidence, such as the use of interviews. We have considered the importance of gathering a range of meaningful data that can provide rich, triangulated insights into the impact of your teaching on learning.

Do:

- have a plan for gathering good evidence that is relevant to your focus and provides rich insights
- plan ways to make the capturing of relevant evidence as easy as possible
- plan to gather evidence from a variety of sources (to enable triangulated analysis).

Don't:

- wait until you need to gather evidence before thinking about how best to do this
- plan to interview learners
- plan to convert rich qualitative data into quantitative data.

FURTHER READING

The following texts may also support you in considering how to gather meaningful data:

Macintyre, C. (2000) *The Art of Action Research in the Classroom.* Abingdon: David Fulton Publishers.

This very readable book provides a practical guide to action research in an accessible way that will be useful to new and aspiring teachers, and other novice researchers. Chapter 4 is particularly relevant in relation to planning how to gather data.

Thomas, G. (2017) *How to Do Your Research Project: A Guide for Students.* 3rd edn. London: Sage.

Chapter 7 of this clear and accessible book provides some rounded guidance on how to choose appropriate approaches for gathering data.

Wilson, E. (2017) 'Data collection', in E. Wilson (ed.), *School-based Research: A Guide for Education Students.* 3rd edn. London: Sage, pp. 175–201.

This chapter provides a helpful guide to planning to collect relevant data for your project.

PART 2

UNDERTAKING YOUR ACTION RESEARCH PROJECT

In Part 2, we aim to provide a reference point for student teachers while undertaking their action research project in a school or another educational setting. We explore issues to guide them about what they should be doing and thinking about in order to enable them to get the most out of their project. We will therefore return to many of the issues addressed in Part 1, but with a focus on action rather than planning. The chapters included in Part 2 are:

Chapter 7: Ethics in action. This chapter returns to the issue of research ethics to provide a review of issues to be addressed early in the placement. It will give further consideration to some of the subtle ethical issues that might arise in the early stages of a project, such as gaining informed consent and ensuring equitable treatment of all children at all times, as well as the importance of abiding by school safeguarding policies and ensuring the welfare of vulnerable individuals.

Chapter 8: 'Capturing' your evidence. This chapter will give consideration to the importance of 'capturing' evidence, particularly as much rich evidence is 'transient' and can easily slip away during the course of a busy school day. The chapter will provide guidance on how to stay focused and the potential benefits of taking an iterative approach so that changes in the focus and methods can be adopted.

Chapter 9: Evaluating as you go. This chapter will encourage new teachers to assess their evidence and evaluate their practice on a regular basis throughout the time of the action research project, rather than waiting until the end to review all the evidence. Guidance will be given on how to 'make sense' of evidence by focusing on detail and strengthening evaluation through reflection on a range of sources of evidence.

7

ETHICS IN ACTION

OBJECTIVES FOR THIS CHAPTER

- To review ethical issues to be addressed early in the project
- To explore some ethical subtleties
- To consider the need to work within school policies to safeguard vulnerable children
- To identify ethical issues to be considered towards the end of the project that contribute to an openness about your enquiry.

SOME ETHICAL ISSUES TO ADDRESS EARLY ON IN THE PROJECT

In this chapter, we will build on the guidance from Chapter 5 to identify those issues that will require attention early in the placement, to consider some of the issues that may need careful consideration throughout the time of the project and to identify some 'end of project' issues. Remember that ethical issues should not be seen as a hurdle but as a way to strengthen the quality of your overall approach, as outlined by Kay (2020: 29–30): 'examining the approaches for gathering and analysing data through an ethical lens in addition to a methodological lens enhances the validity of the research and its conclusions'.

We begin with a review of some of the key issues that should be addressed early in the project.

GATEKEEPERS

A key priority at the outset of the project is to discuss your planned research with key individuals within the school, including your mentor and, most importantly, your headteacher, principal or other relevant senior member of staff. You should explain what your focus is, in relation to the development of your practice, and your personal and professional rationale for this. You should discuss the evidence that you plan to gather and how this relates to any relevant school policies, such as those relating to the use of photographic evidence, audio-recording or photocopies/photographs of children's written or pictorial work. You should also discuss and agree an appropriate approach for informing parents about your action research and seeking their consent.

INFORMED CONSENT FROM PARENTS

It is important to communicate with parents very early in the process and to give them appropriate information about your focus, rationale and, most importantly, the kind of evidence that you plan to gather. Remember that you are not asking for permission to teach the children or young people but seeking consent in relation to the gathering of evidence. Depending on the nature of the evidence that you plan to gather, and guidance from your ethical gatekeepers, you should decide whether you should seek what Thomas (2017: 47) refers to as 'implied consent' from parents or something more rigorous. The difference between 'written consent' and 'implied consent' relates to whether you require parents to sign a form to give their permission for you to include their child in the evidence sample, or whether it would be sufficient to fully inform them of the project and the evidence you plan to gather and invite them to discuss any concerns with you and to withdraw their child from the study if they wish (implied consent). To put it another way, written consent involves the parents giving their permission for their children to be involved in the study, while implied consent assumes that all children will be involved in the sample unless parents express concerns about this and withdraw their child from the sample.

The decision as to whether implied consent is appropriate is normally related to the nature of the evidence to be gathered and, in any case, it is important for parents/legal guardians to be well informed about the project so that they can make a decision about how they should respond. Evidence of a non-contentious and 'everyday' nature (such as copies of children's work) would normally only require implied consent, whereas evidence that is not gathered as part of the day-to-day practice of a teacher and is more personal in nature (such as photographs, audio-recording of interactions) is more likely to require explicit evidence of consent. The decision about this should be made in line with BERA's ethical guidelines, advice from the school or setting and, if the project is part of an award or qualification, the supervising institution.

A sample letter is provided below, which is only a guide and should be edited carefully to suit your particular needs. It is drafted to address the requirements of implied consent but could easily be adapted to include a form for written consent.

If you have any plans to share a summary of your findings in, for example, a published research journal or at a conference, it is worth getting written confirmation of informed consent at an early stage.

DRAFT INTRODUCTORY AND ETHICS LETTER

Edit as appropriate and ensure the school staff are happy with content and approach.

Dear Parent/Carer,

I am writing to introduce myself. I am a PGCE/BEd/BA (QTS) student/trainee teacher and will be undertaking a placement in your child's class throughout the autumn/spring/summer term, taking increasing responsibility for leading the teaching and learning.

As part of my course, I will be undertaking a small research study, focusing on the development of an aspect of my practice as a teacher. The aim of the research is to enable me to understand the impact of my teaching on the children's learning and so improve my teaching. The aspect of my teaching I have chosen to focus on is . . . The children's learning and welfare will be paramount throughout and no child will be unfairly advantaged or disadvantaged as a result of the project.

(Continued)

For the purposes of the research study, in order to understand the impact of my teaching on the children's progress, I will be gathering some evidence related to the children's learning. This will include photocopies of children's work, observational notes, notes of things the children say . . . The evidence will be kept securely and only used for the purposes of my report and will be deleted/destroyed upon successful completion of the module. The report will not be published or made available online. The name of the school will not appear in the report and individual children will not be identified by name.

The project has been discussed with Mr/Miss/Mrs . . . and they support the planned approach. If you have any questions or concerns about the project, or if you would prefer your child to be excluded from the evidence gathered, please let me know.

I am really looking forward to working with your child this term and look forward to meeting you in due course.

Yours faithfully,

INFORMED CONSENT FROM CHILDREN

Thomas (2017: 44) notes that, in considering ethical issues, 'there is a recognition that participants have rights . . . it shouldn't be a question of simply using people and then waving goodbye'. Just as it is important to inform the parents, it is equally important to tell the children or young people about your enquiry and seek their permission for the collection of any evidence that you plan to gather. This should be done in a way that is appropriate to the age of the children or young people and with respect to the children's individual needs and circumstances. For students in secondary schools and colleges, and those in the later years of primary schools, this is likely to mean providing the children with a brief written statement about the purpose of your research, the evidence that you plan to gather, any implications for the young people, and, of course, their right to withdraw (not from the teaching and learning but from the sample in relation to evidence). In the early years and the lower years of primary, it is more likely that a verbal explanation of what you are doing might be appropriate.

BEST PRACTICE FROM THE START

Remind yourself, right from the start of the placement, that you must give of your best to the learners you are working with. Avoid the temptation to do less than your best in the hope that you will be able to demonstrate more improvement over time. Keep in mind, throughout the project, what you are trying to achieve: you are trying to become a better teacher as a result of the focused evaluation of key evidence, so there should be no 'experiments' or 'comparison' of approaches. That is not to say that you should not sometimes try something new as it is good to take risks in your teaching, but this should not be undertaken as an experiment to see 'which works best'.

EVALUATE YOUR OWN PRACTICE ONLY

A key ethical principle of action research is that you should only ever evaluate your own practice and not that of other teachers with whom you work. The purpose of action research is to improve your own practice, not to demonstrate how your practice is better than that of others.

SOME SUBTLETIES AND CHALLENGES

Action research is a complex process and there are some subtle issues and challenges that arise throughout such projects that need to be addressed carefully and responsibly.

FOCUS GROUPS AND EDUCATIONAL DIFFERENTIATION

A focus group can be a useful way of gathering some detailed evidence from a smaller sample than the whole class or group. However, as we discussed in Chapter 5, remember that children in your focus group should not be treated any differently from the rest of

the class and certainly should not experience any advantage or disadvantage as a result of your enquiry. Treating children differently for educational reasons is, of course, acceptable and something that good teachers do every day (we call it differentiation), so if the focus group needs a different approach for teaching and learning reasons that is absolutely fine; in fact, it would be unethical not to aim to meet their learning needs to the best of your ability. Throughout, you should keep an eye out to check that your focus group is not being advantaged in any way, just as much as you should ensure they experience no disadvantage.

INTERVIEWS AND LEARNING CONFERENCES

In many forms of social science research, an interview can be a very rich source of valuable qualitative evidence, providing insights into a social situation or a personal perspective that is difficult to explore in other ways. However, interviews with children or young people are not recommended as part of an action research project, for two main reasons, one ethical and one methodological. The imbalance of power between a teacher and the children or young people in their care means that it would be difficult to avoid coercion: that is, the children or young people will feel under some level of pressure to give certain responses. Some teachers may argue that their relationship with their class is so good that the respondents will be able to comment freely and say exactly what they wish . . . but, however good the relationship, the imbalance of power is a constant, and we should never assume that the children's or young people's responses are entirely honest. This brings us to the methodological objection: as a method of gathering meaningful and valid evidence about your teaching, an interview with a child or group of children in your class is unlikely to yield valid or useful evidence, as they are likely to only tell you what you want to hear (Koshy, 2010).

   Many student teachers are disappointed to learn that interviews are not recommended in action research, as they are keen to gain an insight into the children's experiences of the learning process. One way in which this can be addressed, which is both ethically and methodologically more appropriate than interviews, is through the use of 'learning conferences', in which a teacher meets with an individual or small group (often pairs) of children or young people to review their recent learning, perhaps with reference to some of their written work. The emphasis is on understanding how the learners are progressing, what they have found easy or challenging, things they have or have not understood, and to inform future target setting or planning. From an ethical point of view, this approach is appropriate as it is well aligned with the daily practice of teachers in supporting learning through formative assessment. There is no coercion, as the teacher is not asking any 'leading questions' about their teaching but is instead trying to understand the children's learning. From a methodological point of view, the learning conference is likely to yield some valuable insights into the children's learning with which to inform the teacher's reflections on the effectiveness of their teaching.

Of course, the use of learning conferences does raise another ethical dilemma of its own, as explored in Critical task 7.1.

CRITICAL TASK 7.1

Sarah is teaching a Year 3 class, as her final teaching practice on a BA (QTS) programme. She is undertaking an action research project focused on developing her skills in engaging the children in self-assessment. She wants to find out from the children what they think about the approach she has used for this, but her supervisor has advised against interviewing the children. She decides to undertake some learning conferences with pairs of children from her focus group. These only take 10 minutes or so each, and they give her a really valuable insight into the children's recent learning, the elements they are struggling with, and how they are progressing against their targets. She is really pleased with the outcome of the learning conferences, but she has a nagging ethical concern about the equity of this approach. How might you advise her?

LACK OF CONSENT

One potential challenge may arise if a child, young person or their parent refuses to grant consent for their inclusion in the sample but this should not be seen as highly problematic. Remember that you are not requesting parents' permission to teach their children or offering young people the choice of opting out of your lessons: the consent relates purely to the gathering of evidence in relation to their learning. So, if a particular child is withdrawn from your evidence sample, this should not be greatly problematic and your challenge will be to ensure that this child suffers no disadvantage as a result of being excluded from your data sample.

CONFIDENTIALITY THROUGHOUT

A key ethical principle of all research is that of confidentiality, and this is particularly true of action research in schools and other educational settings. It is usually well understood that the principle of confidentiality applies when writing up a research report, but it is equally important to remember that the principle also applies to your practice throughout the project. You should not discuss specific details of your evidence about specific children or young people outside of the school or setting, except with your tutors or supervisors. It is particularly important not to share any details or evidence through social media.

SAFEGUARDING VULNERABLE PUPILS

It is, of course, essential that you should take particular care over safeguarding vulnerable pupils and the school or setting will have guidelines and policies in place to support you in relation to this. These may relate to the use of photographs or other evidence and it is very important that you discuss these issues carefully with the school. In some cases, it is important for a child or young person's safety that their attendance at a particular institution is not known to certain individuals, so it is essential that their image does not appear in any documents, and that their anonymity is very carefully preserved.

STAYING ALERT TO ETHICAL ISSUES

Throughout the project, you should stay alert to ethical issues and respond to these as they arise. There are sometimes unintended consequences of our actions, issues can be overlooked and, in the dynamic environment of an educational setting, things can change rapidly, so it is important to keep an eye out for ethical issues that may require a thoughtful and respectful response. For example, if a new child joins the class you will need to make a judgement about whether to revise your sample to include them. If your teaching approaches seem not to be effective for a particular child or group, you will need to respond to this. If some children are finding your observations to be unsettling, you will have to adapt your approach to gathering evidence.

CRITICAL TASK 7.2

Caleb is undertaking a secondary PGCE in history. He has been trying to improve the way in which he facilitates rich discussion about key historical concepts. In response to his own evaluations and feedback from his mentor, he has made some small adjustments to his practice and is really pleased with the impact this is having: almost all children have responded well in discussions and this seems to be impacting positively on outcomes for the vast majority of the class in their written responses to tasks.

   What should Caleb's next steps be to ensure that his approach is ethical and develops his practice further?

TOWARDS THE END AND AFTER THE PROJECT

Towards the end of the project, arrange a time to share your findings with colleagues within the school and perhaps with the parents and children, too. This is a way to bring the project to a close through being open about your evidence and findings. This might be towards the end of the project or afterwards, once you have had some time to reflect on your evidence and distil your findings. While it would be great if you could share your key findings with the whole school staff in a development meeting, it is more likely that you will arrange a time to have a cup of coffee with the colleagues you worked most closely with, just to chat through some of the issues that you explored.

Finally, remember to store your evidence securely throughout so that your commitment of confidentiality is maintained. After the project is complete, it is good practice to delete evidence such as audio-recordings from your electronic devices, but it is wise not to delete any data too soon. If you are undertaking your action research project as part of an academic module or course, it is worth waiting until you are sure you have passed before permanently deleting any evidence that you might require if you unfortunately need to resubmit your assignment.

RESPONSE TO CRITICAL TASK 7.1

Sarah's nagging ethical concern is that she has realised that conducting the learning conference with just her focus group means that she is treating them differently from the rest of the class and, as such, almost certainly offering them an educational advantage, as she understands their learning needs more fully and is able to respond to them to develop their learning. Following discussion with colleagues, she decides that she will undertake learning conferences with all children in the class. This will support her understanding of their learning needs and also provide further opportunities to gather useful evidence for her enquiry, although she will retain her original focus group for the purposes of gaining detailed insights into the learning of a group of children over the time of the project.

RESPONSE TO CRITICAL TASK 7.2

Caleb is pleased that almost everyone in the class has responded well to his improved approach to engaging them in rich discussion in his history lessons. He is aware, though, that there are some individual children who are not responding so well and who appear not to be benefitting as much as others. For his next step, he decides to reflect on how he might adapt his practice further to include these 'hard to reach' learners. This is important from an ethical perspective and will also enable him to become a better teacher.

SUMMARY FOR THIS CHAPTER

In this chapter, we have considered some of the ethical issues that require early action during the action research project, such as discussing your plans with the ethical gatekeepers and ensuring the participants and their parents have been provided with good information about the purpose of the research and the evidence that you plan to gather. We have explored some of the subtle ethical issues that need to be given careful consideration, such as managing the implications of using a focus group and how to gain meaningful insights into children's learning without using unethical interviews. We have thought about how to bring the project to a close, demonstrating respect for all parties.

In the next chapter, we will explore how to ensure that you can 'capture' good evidence to inform the detailed evaluation of your practice.

Do:

- discuss your project with appropriate gatekeepers very early in the process
- inform parents about the project and seek their consent
- inform the children in an age-appropriate way
- ensure that no child or group of children is either advantaged or disadvantaged as a result of your action research
- keep data confidential and secure
- be open with the school about your findings.

Don't:

- be lazy about ethics
- include any children in your data sample if their parents have expressed concerns
- talk about any confidential details of your enquiry outside the setting and other appropriate professional contexts
- delete your data too soon.

FURTHER READING

The following texts may also support you in reflecting on ethical issues to be addressed during your project:

Brooks, R., te Riele, K. and Maguire, M. (2014) *Ethics and Education Research*. London: Sage.

Through the use of scenarios and vignettes, this book offers a detailed view of many of the ethical considerations that researchers need to bear in mind when conducting education research.

Jones, M. and Stanley, G. (2008) 'Children's lost voices: ethical issues in relation to undertaking collaborative, practice-based projects involving schools and the wider community', *Educational Action Research*, 16 (1): 31–41.

This interesting article explores some of the challenges and complexities regarding appropriate ethical safeguards for those involved in action research projects.

Stutchbury, K. (2017) 'Ethics in educational research', in E. Wilson (ed.), *School-based Research: A Guide for Education Students*. 3rd edn. London: Sage, pp. 90–102.

This chapter explores ethical issues in a practical way and includes a useful checklist of questions to ask yourself about your enquiry plan.

8

'CAPTURING' YOUR EVIDENCE

OBJECTIVES FOR THIS CHAPTER

- To consider how to 'capture' a range of valuable evidence
- To explore how to capture transient data that can easily slip through your fingers
- To consider the benefits of staying organised and focused
- To think about triangulation and validity when gathering data.

CAPTURING EVIDENCE

In this chapter, we will discuss ways in which you can ensure that you capture appropriate evidence that is relevant to your enquiry, including data that might otherwise slip through your fingers. We will explore the benefits of keeping your evidence well organised, in chronological order, so that you can easily compare sources and explore what they reveal.

Remember that evidence is only of value to you if it is relevant to your stated focus, so it is worth returning to your overarching aim to remind yourself of what you are trying to achieve, and to review your objectives, regularly, to remind yourself of what you are trying to find out. Staying clear on this is important, as it will guide you in your choices about gathering useful evidence.

EVIDENCE THAT IS RELATIVELY EASY TO CAPTURE

Assessment information: At the beginning of an action research enquiry, it may be useful to explore pre-existing assessment evidence about the attainment of the learners, which can provide some insights into their current understanding, knowledge or prior learning experiences. This may be in the form of assessment records, test results or the personal insights and understanding of an experienced teacher. However, it is worth being cautious about the value of this evidence, as it may not provide the kind of detailed insights that would be useful for making judgements about progress over a relatively short period of time.

Copies of work: Children and young people's written or pictorial work is a readily available source of evidence that new and aspiring teachers have easy access to on a daily basis. However, before standing at the photocopier with a pile of books, you should be clear about what you will be looking for in the work and consider whether the data will provide the evidence that you require. You also need to take a cautious approach when using written or pictorial work as evidence, as it is not always a genuine reflection of independent understanding or learning; work that is heavily 'guided' or that was undertaken in collaboration with others, or where one learner has replicated the work of another, will clearly not reveal the real learning of individuals. It is worth annotating copied work as soon as possible with important information about, for example, the level of independence with which it was completed.

Evaluation: Your own professional evaluation of your practice is an important source of valuable evidence and this is often forgotten or under-valued. This may be in the form of lessons or daily evaluations or a reflective diary, the last of which Wilson (2017: 177) recommends as an 'effective way of keeping control of the information your research generates', however you choose to capture your reflections on your practice, it is important to do so regularly and to try to write these as soon as possible after the teaching episode they relate to. Evaluations can, and should, be undertaken both before and after reviewing other evidence about the learning. Evaluation undertaken immediately after a lesson will enable you to capture your 'on-the-spot' reflections on how it went and note any particular incidents or insights that seem important at the time. Further evaluation, undertaken as part of your review of other evidence, will enable you to reflect on the range of evidence about the learning experiences of the children or young people and identify some specific actions that might inform the development of your teaching in the next lesson. We will explore this further in the following chapter.

Third-party feedback: Remember to ask for feedback on your teaching, and the learning you facilitate, from your mentor or another member of teaching staff. It is helpful to be specific about the aspect of your practice that you are particularly focusing on and the kind of issues you are addressing or finding challenging. Most mentors will be very happy to offer specific advice, tailored to your development priorities, so be proactive about asking for feedback and arranging observations related to your action research enquiry.

Photographs: It can be useful to take photos of specific aspects of children's work or even of the children themselves at work; it is important to date these and to make some relevant comment about them in your evaluation of the lesson. Some caution should be taken in relation to the use of photographs: clearly there are ethical considerations when photographing children or young people and, as discussed in Chapter 6, it is also important to consider whether a photograph will provide any meaningful insight into the learning, as a picture may not do much more than demonstrate what the learners *did*, which is not the same thing as what they *learnt*.

TRANSIENT DATA

Transient data is all the 'stuff' that happens in the course of teaching and learning that it is difficult to capture and of which there is no obvious or easy record. These are episodes that occur, briefly, in time and space and then are gone for ever, but some elements of them can be 'captured' for analysis and reflection.

Spoken words: Things that children or young people say are often very revealing and yet so easily forgotten in the busy and dynamic life in schools and other educational settings, so it is important to plan how and when you are going to capture this transient data. As we discussed in Chapter 6, while audio-recording of classroom interactions is a valuable way of making a record of what is said in the classroom, it is not without its challenges, such as issues of clarity and background noise, and the time required to listen carefully to recordings and transcribe the important parts. Wragg (2012: 71) notes that teachers and pupils may 'talk at 100 to 150 words a minute', so transcribing even a short discussion can take some time. So remember that handwritten notes of things you hear are an absolutely acceptable form of data, so long as their main limitation is recognised: any notes jotted down as children speak cannot be relied on as a verbatim (word-for-word) record, and should not be presented as such. However, making handwritten notes while also teaching can be tricky, so remember to make this as easy for yourself as possible, by using pre-prepared grids, pro forma or tables so that you can jot down noteworthy observations in an organised way. It is particularly important to use a pro forma of some kind if asking colleagues, such as teaching assistants, to make assessment records for you during the lesson, as the form should indicate very clearly what kind of evidence you are looking for.

Observation: Similarly, find time in your teaching schedule to stand back and observe the learners at work, noting the detail of what they do and how they do it; some teachers find it useful to use Post-its to capture relevant notes that can easily be added to other evidence. In making these observational notes, you should avoid, as much as possible, making judgements about what the observations might mean, and focus on what you see. For example, you might want to write that 'John seemed confused by the work' but it is better just to note the behaviour: 'John stares at the wall and scratches his head'. Of course, this could mean that he is confused by the work, but it might also mean several other things: perhaps he is bored, worried about something that happened at the weekend, wondering when it will be break time or whether he should ask for permission to go to the toilet. It is better to have a good record of what you observed rather than a record of your interpretation of events. You can reflect on this evidence later, along with other relevant evidence, to help make an informed and more objective judgement.

Formative assessment: Other transient evidence may relate to formative assessment strategies adopted within lessons, such as the use of 'thumbs up', showing whiteboards or number fans or even a show of hands or a vote. This is the kind of evidence where it can be useful to ask a colleague, such as a teaching assistant, to help you with capturing the children's responses, or to photograph a child's whiteboard working.

With all kinds of data, and particularly with transient data, it is important to build the process of capturing the evidence into your lesson plans. Identify when there will be good opportunities to make observational notes, or when it is most likely that you will want to capture the words spoken in your lesson. You may even include some empty boxes on your lesson plan for noting down children's responses to a problem, or how many of them voted for a particular response to an assessment question. The better prepared you are for capturing your data, the more meaningful data you will capture.

Throughout, in gathering transient data, remember the importance of *authenticity*. This means that, when presenting your evidence in the analysis, it should be very obvious that the evidence that you are drawing on is genuine and reflects your ethical commitment to being truthful and open about all aspects of your enquiry.

CRITICAL TASK 8.1

Julie, a BEd primary student teacher, made some notes based on her observations during her recent mathematics lesson. The focus for her development was her use of questioning to develop the young people's mathematical reasoning. After reading her observation notes, suggest ways in which she might make these more useful to her action research enquiry in subsequent lessons.

Good start: Class settled well. A few good answers to my questions, demonstrating some good understanding; J, C and G give thoughtful responses to my questions about the area of a circle. My questions are more focused today. Individual work: children working hard and most seem to be making progress – they're happy and co-operative – even M is on task.

STAYING ORGANISED

It may sound obvious and even patronising to suggest that it would be a good idea to stay organised throughout your project, but failure to do so can make the process more complicated and angst-ridden than it needs to be.

Make sure that, right from the start, you keep evidence clearly labelled with names and dates, in chronological order; keep related evidence together along with the focused evaluations that link it all. Later on, in your analysis and written account, you may choose to use pseudonyms for the children or young people, but at this stage it is probably best to use their real names when labelling data or referring to them in your evaluations, so that you do not get confused about who is who; of course, you must ensure that your approach to labelling is in line with school policy. Do, however, think ahead to the stage when the evidence will need to be redacted to hide names and any other identifying features; small written labelling at this stage will be easier to cover later.

Aim to keep up to date with writing up your evaluations and other field notes. These should be done as soon as possible after the lesson or episode you are reflecting on, and should include the date, the particular focus of the evaluation and, perhaps most importantly, the specific action points that arise from your reflections. We will explore this further in the next chapter.

Aim to stay focused throughout your project. If you are not entirely clear what you are trying to achieve, it is easy to gather masses of data that may or may not be useful or relevant to your focus. Keep your objectives in mind throughout, and use these as the guide as to which data will be valuable to you.

A final word about being organised: do not leave it too late to start gathering data. The secret to avoiding this problem lies in being very clear about what you are trying to achieve and about the data you need to gather. If you are not clear about this, a kind of inertia can develop in which it becomes difficult to get started, so if you are experiencing this kind of difficulty, review your enquiry plan to ensure that you are confident about what you are doing and talk your plans through with someone . . . and then get started.

CASE STUDY 8.1

Andre is a PGCE primary student teacher and is undertaking his final teaching placement in a Reception class. In the early stages of the placement, Andre found it difficult to adapt to the play-based approach taken in his class, as it was such a contrast to the more formal approaches adopted in his previous placement, in a Year 2 class. Recognising the importance of developing effective pedagogy for teaching in the early years, Andre decided to focus his action research project on developing his skills in extending children's mathematical learning, through his engagement in their child-initiated play. He defined clear enquiry objectives, engaged with some relevant literature to develop his knowledge and understanding of this focus, and discussed the ethical considerations with his PGCE tutor before commencing his enquiry.

Three weeks before the end of his placement, Andre contacted his PGCE tutor, concerned that he had gathered 'very little useful evidence'. In a telephone discussion, Andre shared that he didn't have copies of children's work, 'as they don't do much writing', and he therefore felt that he didn't have evidence of his impact on learning. While children's work (written and pictorial) can be a valuable source of evidence, it is certainly not the only source that can demonstrate impact on learners and learning. Andre's tutor reminded him that the use of observation is an integral part of effective early years practice, so not only would observations be a useful source of evidence, he would also be developing an important skill. Andre noted that he had been jotting down some of the things both he and the children said during their play, where he felt that this was relevant to their mathematical learning, but he was worried that this wasn't good evidence as he hadn't audio-recorded it. His tutor reassured him that, as long as he was honest about how he had collected this form of evidence, and recognised that it wouldn't be a verbatim record, this could indeed be a very valuable potential source of evidence, so long as it provided insights into Andre's impact on the children's mathematical learning. They discussed how he might plan and prepare to capture spoken words in a more organised manner during the remaining time in the placement, perhaps by preparing a pro forma with his planned interactions already noted and spaces for recording the children's responses and his own spontaneous interactions. Andre's tutor reminded him to ensure that his own evaluations were included as part of his collection of evidence and encouraged him to ask for more feedback from his mentor in relation to his focus. As the children in his class had open access to paper, pencils, individual whiteboards and so on during their play, Andre also resolved to be alert to capturing any spontaneous written or pictorial records of their learning.

STAYING FLEXIBLE AND RESPONSIVE

One of the great things about action research is that there are many ways to approach it and these can be developed in real time during the project. You may, for example, think of different ways in which to gather your evidence, particularly if, as your project develops, you need to gain new insights into particular aspects of the children's or young people's learning. For example, if focusing on engaging learners in the process of self-assessment, you may have gathered valuable information, from their written work, about how well the learners were engaging with the process of self-assessment, but realise, after a few episodes, that what you really need to understand is how this is impacting on their progress, so analysis of their work will be valuable.

(In being responsive with gathering evidence, remember to avoid the temptation to engage in interviews or questionnaires, as these are unlikely to yield valuable insights and may be unethical; see Chapters 5 and 7. If an interesting issue has arisen that you wish to explore more fully, find other ways to gain insights into the situation.)

In a similar way, you should be prepared to amend the guiding objectives of your enquiry, if you find that they are not tight enough, or too tightly defined, or do not reflect the issues that you are finding most interesting and useful in the development of your practice. In action research nothing is set in stone, and taking an iterative approach can be very valuable in squeezing as much from the process as possible.

TRIANGULATION AND VALIDITY

In Chapter 6, we explored the idea of triangulation, which relates to looking at a social situation from more than one angle through gathering data of different kinds or from different sources. During your study, you should seek opportunities to triangulate your data, as different aspects of evidence that all 'point' to the same thing increase the validity of your analysis and the confidence in your findings. However, it is also important to look out for 'negative evidence' (Evans, 2017: 213), as it is valuable to interrogate interesting issues or anomalies that arise, when the data does not seem to all point the same way. Anomalies are interesting in all research but can easily be overlooked (sometimes even deliberately so), and in action research it is often the anomalies that are important to understanding the detail of your practice and to improving the impact of your teaching. To continue the example from above: perhaps the analysis of your evidence reveals that all of the learners are engaging well with the self-assessment process and your recently developed analysis of the learners' progress reveals that nearly all are making good progress as a result of their engagement. It would be tempting to congratulate yourself and move on, but there is an anomaly here which is nagging at you: some learners (it might be only one or two) are, apparently, using the self-assessment process yet not making the expected progress and so the next steps in your action research enquiry become clear, as you will choose to explore what is 'going on' with this situation and see how you can ensure all learners can make good progress.

While gathering your data, it is worth planning and being clear about how you will analyse it: be clear about what you will look for, and even begin to think about how the analysis might look in the written report.

CRITICAL TASK 8.2

Tim, a PGCE primary student, started his action research with a particular focus on meeting individual needs through appropriate differentiation but now, with just four weeks to go until the end of his placement, he has realised that the use of resources to support differentiation is emerging as an important element of practice for reflection and development. He has begun to explore how to differentiate through effective resourcing and is becoming aware that this might be a good focus for his enquiry. How would you advise Tim to develop his action research project?

RESPONSE TO CRITICAL TASK 8.1

Julie has asked you to review her observation notes. How might they be made more useful to her action research enquiry?

> Good start: Class settled well. A few good answers to my questions, demonstrating some good understanding; J, C and G give thoughtful responses to my questions about the area of a circle. My questions are more focused today. Individual work: children working hard and most seem to be making progress – they're happy and co-operative – even M is on task.

Julie's observation notes are not sufficiently detailed to be very useful to her. For example, it would have been beneficial to note what her 'more focused' questions were, what the 'good answers' were and which specific learners gave which responses. Before teaching her next mathematics lesson, Julie should decide whether she plans to audio-record an appropriate part of the lesson, in order to capture all the questions and responses, or to prepare a table or grid to enable her to more easily note the responses of individual learners. She may be able to prepare this with her pre-planned questions already filled in, and with some spaces for any spontaneous questions. If possible, she may seek support from a classroom colleague to make some observational notes for her.

RESPONSE TO CRITICAL TASK 8.2

Tim has asked for your advice. He started his action research with a particular focus on meeting individual needs through appropriate differentiation, but now, with just four weeks to go until the end of his placement, he has realised that the use of resources to support differentiation is emerging as an important element of practice for reflection and development.

It's not too late for Tim to change or refine his focus, if the issue of developing his resourcing is genuinely emerging as a valuable focus for his development. If this is what he wants to do, he should revisit his enquiry objectives and develop a really clear focus; at this stage, he does not have the time to work it out as he goes along. Once he has identified some clear objectives, he should make a clear plan for gathering meaningful data that will ensure that he can undertake some serious analysis of the effectiveness of his use of resources. He will already have some relevant evidence from his previous work on differentiation, so he should review this to see what can be learnt from it about how his use of resources has already developed. If he can find the time, he should also engage in some reading about resourcing.

SUMMARY FOR THIS CHAPTER

In this chapter, we have considered how the action researching new teacher can capture good evidence, which is central to the evaluative process of an effective and valuable action research enquiry. We have explored the importance of gathering a range of data, including some that is harder to capture, and the need to keep this well organised. We have explored the benefits of maintaining a flexible approach, as your development priorities change in response to circumstances or your own learning. Finally, we have given a reminder to have an explicit focus on triangulation to increase the validity of the enquiry and to not be afraid of anomalies but to seek them out and explore their meaning. In the next chapter, we will consider how to make the most of your evidence through regular evaluation.

Do:

- be clear about the evidence that you will need to gather in order to shed light on the focus area of your practice
- gather meaningful evidence regularly
- capture transient data
- write up evaluation, observation and other field notes promptly
- ask for third-party feedback
- explore anomalies
- be prepared to review, tweak or amend your objectives in response to changing circumstances within the school or setting or your changing professional development priorities.

Don't:

- gather irrelevant evidence that does not help you to focus on your practice
- be afraid of conflicting evidence
- leave it all until the last week.

FURTHER READING

The following texts may also support you in considering how to capture meaningful and relevant data during your study:

Holliday, A. (2016) *Doing and Writing Qualitative Research*. 3rd edn. London: Sage.

This book provides a really clear guide to the process of moving from rich qualitative data to purposeful presentation of evidence in a written account. Chapter 4 relates to gathering relevant and meaningful data.

Lin, Y. (2016) 'Collecting qualitative data', in I. Palaiologou, D. Needham and T. Male (eds), *Doing Research in Education: Theory and Practice*. London: Sage, pp. 156–76.

This chapter provides some guidance on types of data and how to manage data effectively.

Roche, M. (2011) 'Creating a dialogical and critical classroom: reflection and action to improve practice', *Educational Action Research*, 19 (3): 327–43.

This inspiring article tells the story of one teacher's journey from didactic instructor to dialogic facilitator and includes some great insights into how the author was open with her students about the data she was gathering and the impact that this had on their responses.

9

EVALUATING AS YOU GO

OBJECTIVES FOR THIS CHAPTER

- To consider the importance of evaluating as you go and how this relates to action research
- To explore how to make effective use of evidence to support analysis of the children's learning and evaluation of your own practice
- To consider how to use evidence and reading to improve your practice.

THE IMPORTANCE OF EVALUATING AS YOU GO

In this chapter, we will consider the need to evaluate 'as you go' and explore why this is important. We will also consider how to undertake such evaluation, ensuring that this is firmly evidence-based. We will explore the role of literature to inform your evaluation.

Think back to what you learnt in Chapter 1 about the purpose and nature of action research. Hopefully, as advised in Chapter 4, you have also read more widely about action research as an approach to improving your own practice as a teacher. Unlike many other forms of research, where analysis of evidence and evaluation occur after the enquiry is complete, action research involves cycles of planning, implementation, gathering data and reflection on the evidence, in order to inform the planning and implementation of the next cycle. So, 'actions' occur during the enquiry, rather than afterwards. This approach enables you to make adaptations to your practice, reflect on the impact of these and make further adaptations to further refine your practice.

Whether you are a student teacher or a new teacher, evaluation is probably very familiar. You are likely to have written lesson evaluations and/or evaluations focusing on specific aspects of your practice on a regular basis during teaching placements. You are likely to have also evaluated your progress in relation to the *Teachers' Standards* on a regular basis. As Ewens (2014: 71) identifies, 'judging the success of your teaching, and your pupils' learning, is obviously an important professional activity' and even the most experienced teachers engage in regular evaluation, although it may be more of a mental activity, rather than a written one. As part of everyday practice, evaluation can sometimes be viewed as the last step in the chain: planning – teaching – evaluation. When it is viewed in this way, evaluation tends to have limited impact on our practice (and therefore on children's learning). However, according to Lowe and Harris (2018), if you view evaluation as the link between one chain and the next, where evaluation informs the planning and teaching of the next chain, it is likely to have far more impact, and this is exactly the role that evaluation should play in an action research enquiry. The evaluation that you undertake throughout your enquiry is likely to be much more explicit and robust than evaluation you have carried out previously and is therefore likely to improve your evaluation in everyday practice.

When evaluating your lessons previously, you may have focused on the lesson as a whole or as a number of elements. Evaluating as part of an action research enquiry requires you to only judge the effectiveness of your teaching in relation to your enquiry focus, so that you can then use this to inform the planning of your approach to your specific enquiry focus in the next cycle. If your enquiry focus is, for example, developing your effective use of resources to support Year 9 pupils in their understanding of forces, your evaluation needs to focus on judging the effectiveness of your use of resources in that particular cycle, so that you can adapt your practice with regard to the use of resources in the next cycle, with the aim of further enhancing your skills in this aspect of learning and teaching.

LAYERED EVALUATION OF PRACTICE

Within this book, we suggest that there are layers to evaluating your practice effectively and these are summarised in the diagram below:

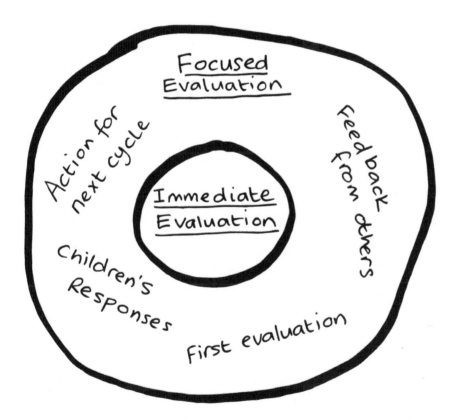

The first layer of evaluation (in the centre of the diagram) is that which you carry out immediately, or very soon, after the lesson. It is likely that, at this point, you will not have had a chance to engage with all of the evidence. For example, if you have audio-recorded the session, you will not have had the opportunity to listen to or transcribe the recording. You have probably not marked or even seen all of the children's work. It is unlikely that you have had the chance to receive feedback from any other adults present during the lesson. So, the first layer of evaluation cannot be described as being fully evidence-based.

However, it is still important to undertake and produce a written record while the lesson is still fresh in your mind. You were part of the 'action' and therefore you are likely to have some thoughts or feelings about your effectiveness in relation to your enquiry focus. Capture these, together with any specific things that you noted about particular children or particular moments in the lesson, ensuring that they are tightly related to your enquiry focus. This should be a relatively quick task and one you should not agonise over, not least because teachers are very busy people and you are likely to need to move quickly on to your next lesson, extra-curricular activity or break duty.

The second layer of evaluation is very different. It is more time-consuming and will be firmly based on analysis of all of the evidence available. It is therefore important to leave sufficient time between cycles to undertake this second layer; as it is such an important part of the process, it is very helpful to allocate, in advance, a specific date, time and place in which to undertake it, rather than trying to squeeze it into your already busy schedule. Before beginning, you need to gather together all of the evidence generated in this cycle, which might include, for example, planning documents, children's work (you need to have marked it), a transcript (or other record) of oral contributions (yours and the children's), assessment records, written feedback from others, field notes, 'rough' observations noted during the lesson; it should also include your first layer evaluation.

ANALYSING THE EVIDENCE

In evaluating the effectiveness of your practice, you need to start by considering the children's learning; as Hattie (2012: 189) phrases it, 'know thy impact'. Your hunch may be that your modelling, for example, was excellent, but if the children have not made progress in their learning, then this is unlikely to be true. You should therefore sift the evidence, firstly locating sources that contain, or might contain, evidence of the children's learning.

If, as is often helpful, you have selected a focus group, start by considering the evidence relating to these particular children. Be clear about what you are looking for evidence of; you need to look for evidence which demonstrates that a child now knows/understands/ can do something new, or that their knowledge/understanding/skill has developed/ increased/improved. One of the benefits of always considering the same children is that it allows you to identify progress over time. You may present evidence and analyse it to demonstrate that, for example, Child B knows that plants need water in order to grow; without evidence of progress over time, one might ask whether Child B actually already knew that and whether or not, therefore, Child B made progress in their learning. Remember that children's oral contributions may provide just as much insight into their learning as their written work does, particularly in the case of younger children or reluctant writers. You also need to consider the scope and context of your enquiry. If your intention was to develop the effectiveness of your feedback to support the development of children's compositional skills in writing poetry, evidence of progress in their handwriting or spelling is not useful to you. As you are analysing the evidence, you may find it helpful to highlight, annotate, add Post-its or colour code, as a record of your analysis.

Establishing that learning has taken place is not an easy task. You need to interrogate the evidence carefully and this may involve some double checking and a critical approach. For example, it may be evident from your transcript that Sophie was unable to identify any of the physical features of the village in Mexico that you are studying in geography, yet her written work includes an accurate list of all of the main physical features. You need to consider the possibilities (for example, whether Sophie copied from another child, or whether an adult supported Sophie's group and the list recorded was generated by the group as a whole) and investigate these as you seek to understand this apparent anomaly. Similarly, if another adult has provided you with assessment records for the group(s) they worked with, indicating which assessment criteria each child met, check whether the other evidence supports the assessment judgements made. Clarify the level of support given by the adult and how the group worked, so that you are clear as to whether responses are collaborative or individual. Remember the importance of triangulation, as discussed in Chapter 6. You can feel more secure about your analysis of the evidence when different types of data and/or data from different sources are 'in agreement'; where they disagree, this provides more detailed insight into the complexities of teaching and learning.

While you may have a focus group and therefore have more evidence relating to these particular children or young people, it is important to consider, in an evidence-based manner, whether the progress made by the focus group is representative of the class as a whole. If not, you need to consider why this might be the case and whether there are any changes that you might need to make. In particular, you need to consider whether your actions might have advantaged (or disadvantaged) the focus group in some way, compared to the rest of the class. As you will remember from Chapters 5 and 7, it is not ethical to treat the children in your focus group differently from the rest of the class (except, of course, as part of educational differentiation which is normal classroom practice).

Once you have established the learning (or not) that has taken place, you then need to engage with the other data sources and look for evidence that directly links the learning to your practice, and specifically to your enquiry focus. This is more challenging than identifying evidence of learning, as teaching is complex and there will be many factors in every lesson which contribute to its success. So although you may have been focusing on, for example, your questioning, it is highly likely that your approaches to differentiation, behaviour management, use of resources, deployment of support staff, use of AfL, and so on, have all contributed to the impact on pupils' learning. Try not to worry about this too much: you are not looking for definitive proof that your questioning had the most significant impact on the pupils' learning; you are looking for evidence that suggests it was one of a number of important factors that impacted on the learning. It is not possible to completely separate your enquiry focus from the other elements of your practice.

It is important to note where and in which ways children did not learn what you intended or if they did not make progress at all in your lesson. You need to be honest about that and consider why it might be the case. Sometimes there is a fundamental issue, which may be entirely unrelated to your enquiry focus, such as identifying an inappropriate learning objective from the outset, or sometimes there is a combination of issues which, together, have impacted negatively on children's progress; your enquiry focus might be one of the issues, so it is important to try to 'unpick' what went wrong. Similarly, seek to understand the reasons for any anomalies. It is very pleasing when the vast majority of the class make significant progress during a lesson, but the highly effective teacher will spend time pondering on the minority that did not. The highly effective teacher will consider potential reasons for this, drawing upon evidence to support their thinking. In particular, they will seek to establish how significant their enquiry focus was in relation to the impact on this minority.

In Chapter 1, we explored some potential limitations of action research, including its subjective nature and the notion that qualitative evidence is open to interpretation; as we pointed out, all evidence is open to interpretation. It is important to be aware of these potential limitations at all stages of the enquiry, but particularly at this stage, and to be tentative in your interpretation of evidence. You must seek to analyse the evidence in a balanced way, being honest and open-minded throughout, even when this challenges your thinking or expectations. In addition to triangulating your evidence, it can be very helpful to have a 'critical friend', someone with whom you can share your evidence and discuss your own interpretations of it. They may be able to offer different interpretations of the same evidence, which you have perhaps not considered, or have discounted because they did not match your expectations. As McNiff and Whitehead (2005: 11) suggest, critical friends 'can help you bring . . . issues to the surface'.

CRITICAL TASK 9.1

Chris is undertaking his final placement as part of his School Direct PGCE secondary course in modern foreign languages. One of the targets he has identified is to improve his written feedback to pupils and he has decided to undertake an action research enquiry to help him address this target.

After one cycle, Chris is particularly interested to note that one child's work shows increased use of the key French vocabulary he has been teaching recently. He remembers that his written feedback on a piece of this child's work last week asked the child to 'try to use more of the new words we have been using in class'.

What would you advise Chris to do next in relation to analysing the children's learning?

EVALUATING YOUR EFFECTIVENESS

Once you have carefully analysed all of your evidence in a balanced manner, you will then be in a position to evaluate your effectiveness in relation to your enquiry focus, remembering that when you make judgements about your practice, these should be primarily based upon the impact that you had on learning. If you followed the advice given in Chapter 4, it is likely that you approached the planning and teaching of even the first cycle having developed your knowledge and understanding of the key factors involved in the effective practice of your enquiry focus through engaging with relevant literature. It is therefore likely that some of your judgements will be relatively positive, identifying what went well, based on thorough analysis of the evidence. Some of your judgements will identify what went less well or what could be further improved; again, you must ensure that the evidence is in alignment with these judgements, rather than a hunch.

Coming to judgements is not, however, the end of the process of evaluating your effectiveness. As discussed earlier in this chapter, evaluation has the most impact when it links

one teaching sequence to the next, so it is important to conclude the process of evaluation with some action planning for the next cycle. You need to decide how you intend
to adapt your practice in relation to your enquiry focus in the next lesson(s). This should
not be a case of plucking an approach or strategy out of the air; decisions should be
made taking full account of your evidence-based evaluation and should be informed by
knowledge. It is strongly recommended that you return to the literature at this point, or
at least to the records you created during your reading, in order to remind yourself of the
key factors that you identified as being significant to effective practice in relation to your
enquiry focus. Based on your evaluation, you need to carefully consider what is likely to
have the most significant impact on your practice at this stage; it would be impossible
to focus on everything at the same time, so you need to be selective, and it is often better
to identify one highly relevant and attainable target that is likely to have a good impact
on learning than three or four targets that are not likely to make much difference in your
teaching.

CASE STUDY 9.1

Imagine that you have been focusing on your use of questions in your teaching. Your
evidence may indicate that, in your most recent lesson, you planned and asked more
open questions than you did previously, which, based on your reading, you believe to be
a positive thing. However, the evidence also indicates that the pupils did not respond to
these questions as you had hoped. Discussion with your critical friend supports your view
that the questions were pitched appropriately for children of this age and attainment.
When you return to the mind map you created as a record of your reading, you remember
the impact that wait-time or thinking time had for others and realise that you gave your
pupils almost no time to think before expecting them to answer your open questions. You
therefore decide to continue to plan and ask open questions, pitched at a similar level to
those in this lesson, but decide to introduce and use thinking time; one literature source
suggests that five seconds is an appropriate length of time, so you decide to do that in
the next lesson. You discuss your plan with your critical friend, who agrees that, based
on the analysis of the evidence and your evaluation of your practice, this seems like a
sensible course of action.

After the next cycle, the evidence indicates that introducing thinking time has been
valuable; more children were willing to respond to your open questions and the quality of
the children's responses improved, with most children providing extended responses and
justifying their answers. However, there is also some evidence that indicates that five seconds is not always appropriate; sometimes it appeared to be too short, as there were one
or two questions that many children struggled to answer, and at other times it appeared
to be too long, as the teaching assistant noted that several children seemed to know the
answers straight away and were able to offer an appropriate response to your question.

You decide to look more closely at your questions and notice that, although all were open, some offered more cognitive challenge than others. On revisiting your notes from reading, you recognise that, when five seconds of thinking time seemed too short, the questions required higher-order thinking skills, whereas others, particularly those when five seconds of thinking time seemed too long, required lower levels of thinking. You decide that you need to read more about thinking skills before planning your next steps, in order to better understand the challenge provided by questions requiring different types of thinking and how this might relate to thinking time.

As can be seen from Case study 9.1, returning to your reading is crucial in order both to help you understand 'what is going on' and to help you to identify which action(s) might be useful in further developing your practice. You might find, as in the example above, that you need to engage in further reading. Remember, though, to return to your enquiry focus and enquiry objectives frequently, to ensure that you are not becoming 'sidetracked'. As outlined in the previous chapter, it may be appropriate to amend your objectives during the enquiry, but this should be a conscious decision, rather than as a result of unintentionally straying from your intended path.

DECIDING WHEN A CYCLE IS 'COMPLETE'

One potentially tricky aspect of undertaking action research is deciding when one cycle is 'complete' and a new cycle should 'begin'. It is helpful to keep in mind that cycles are somewhat artificial and there is not necessarily a single 'right time' to draw one to a close and start the next. As the researcher at the centre of your own study, you decide when you have made sufficient progress with your practice, in relation to your specific focus, to enable you to identify new, developmental targets.

When deciding whether a cycle has run its course, it is helpful to refer to the critical framework you devised as a result of your engagement with the research literature. From your reading, you may have identified four or five features or aspects of effective practice, in relation to your focus. You should not expect to be brilliant at each of these straight away, so, when reviewing your evidence, these should help you to reflect on what went well and what might be improved. The key questions to ask are:

Have I made progress with any of these features of effective practice?

If so, which aspect(s) have I found most challenging or made the least progress in?

Is it possible to identify a specific target or two to improve my teaching?

RESPONSE TO CRITICAL TASK 9.1

Chris is undertaking an action research enquiry with the aim of improving his written feedback to pupils. After one cycle, he is particularly interested to note that one child's work shows increased use of the key French vocabulary he has been teaching recently. He remembers that his written feedback on a piece of this child's work last week asked the child to 'try to use more of the new words we have been using in lessons'. We asked you to advise Chris on what he should do next.

Hopefully, you will have noted that Chris needs to interrogate his evidence more fully. He needs to establish whether this child worked independently. He should look for other evidence to corroborate the notion that this child is now making more use of the new French vocabulary that he has recently taught and that this is due, at least in part, to the written feedback he gave. Chris needs to remember that one child acting on his feedback out of a class of 30 is not particularly convincing, and he should therefore look for evidence that his written feedback has directly impacted on the learning of other children. He should analyse all of the evidence he has from this cycle, in a critical and balanced manner, including reminding himself of the approach he took to providing written feedback and to engaging pupils with it. Chris should then seek to evaluate the effectiveness of his written feedback and plan his next steps; hopefully, as you read on through this chapter, you identified the significance of Chris returning to his reading.

SUMMARY FOR THIS CHAPTER

In this chapter, we have considered how important it is, during an action research enquiry, to evaluate your practice as you go, so that you can plan your next steps. We have explored the need to ensure that the evaluation is based firmly on thorough and balanced analysis of the evidence, with particular emphasis on the impact on pupils' learning. We have considered the importance of triangulation and the potential value of discussing your evaluation with a critical friend, in order to ensure that your research is as robust as possible. We have explored the importance of returning to literature, both to support the evaluation process and to support you in planning the next cycle.

Do:

- capture a 'first layer' evaluation immediately after the lesson
- recognise the importance of evaluating as you go and allocate time for the process
- gather all of the available evidence before undertaking your 'second layer' evaluation
- carefully analyse all of the evidence in a balanced way, being open to unexpected outcomes
- ensure that your analysis focuses primarily on the pupils' learning
- triangulate your evidence, so that your claims are more secure

- consider working with a critical friend
- come to some judgements about the effectiveness of your practice (in relation to the enquiry focus and based on the evidence)
- plan specific targets for action in the next cycle (in relation to the enquiry focus and based on your evaluation)
- return to your reading.

Don't:

- rush the analysis and evaluation (or worse, miss it altogether) after each cycle
- jump to conclusions without considering all of the evidence
- discount the unexpected
- forget all of the knowledge and understanding you developed through your engagement with literature.

FURTHER READING

The following texts may also support you in evaluating as you go:

Macintyre, C. (2000) *The Art of Action Research in the Classroom.* Abingdon: David Fulton Publishers.

This accessible text includes a chapter on 'Analysing the data'. In particular, the author focuses on the need to consider all possible explanations when analysing the evidence, summarising this very neatly.

McNiff, J. and Whitehead, J. (2005) *Action Research for Teachers: A Practical Guide.* Abingdon: David Fulton Publishers.

Chapter 3 of this useful text, 'Putting your plans into action', provides guidance and support for undertaking a reflective action research process.

Trauth-Nare, A. and Buck, G. (2011) 'Using reflective practice to incorporate formative assessment in a middle school science classroom: a participatory action research study', *Educational Action Research*, 19 (3): 379–98.

This inspiring article emphasises the value of reflection and of engaging in discussion with a critical friend after each cycle of the action research enquiry. It also explores the benefits of sharing your enquiry and modelling the reflective process with pupils.

PART 3

WRITING YOUR ACTION RESEARCH PROJECT REPORT

In Part 3, we aim to provide guidance on writing an effective report on the action research project as a concise and evidence-rich dissertation or assignment. Each section of the report will be considered in turn, with guidance as to the key elements to include and how to ensure the work is academically sound. Throughout this part, examples based on real assignments will help to illustrate points about effective writing, to ensure that the finished report reflects the quality of the action research enquiry. The chapters included in Part 3 are:

Chapter 10: Writing the introduction to your action research report. This chapter provides guidance on communicating a clear rationale for the action research enquiry and on how to decide which aspects of contextual information are important to include in the account. It emphasises the need for alignment throughout the written report, based on clear and appropriate objectives, which should be established in the introduction.

Chapter 11: Writing the literature review. This chapter aims to support student teachers to understand how to engage critically with published research and other literature sources, through exploring their validity and reliability or through comparing sources, and offers guidance on suitable structures for the review.

Chapter 12: Writing the enquiry design or research plan. This chapter provides guidance on how to succinctly present an appropriate enquiry design or research plan, focusing closely on the specific approaches taken to gather and interpret evidence, with consideration of their potential strengths and limitations. The chapter offers guidance on how a student teacher can demonstrate their effective management of ethical issues through their written report.

Chapter 13: Writing the implementation and analysis section. This chapter provides guidance on how to write an evidence-rich, analytical, evaluative and concise account of the enquiry and how tentative conclusions can be drawn. The emphasis is on the importance of self-criticality to improve teaching to support improved outcomes for learners.

Chapter 14: Writing the conclusion to your action research report. This chapter provides guidance on how to write a clear and effective summary to the written report, with consideration of how to summarise findings, evaluate the relative strengths and limitations of the study, and reflect on the impact of the enquiry on the development of teaching skills.

10

WRITING THE INTRODUCTION TO YOUR ACTION RESEARCH REPORT

OBJECTIVES FOR THIS CHAPTER

- To explore the content for the introductory chapter of your written report
- To consider how to communicate the context and rationale for the study
- To emphasise the need for alignment throughout the study, based on clear and appropriate objectives outlined in the introduction
- To consider the importance of the introduction in setting the tone for the report.

THE CONTENT AND PURPOSE OF THE INTRODUCTION

In this chapter, we will consider how to write an effective introduction to a written report of an action research enquiry. The introduction is an important chapter or section of the report, as it sets out to enable the reader (and marker, if an assessed piece of work) to understand five key issues that frame the rest of the report:

1. the specific focus for the enquiry
2. the personal and professional rationale for the enquiry
3. the wider rationale and context
4. the local context
5. the clear objectives that guided the enquiry and to which all sections of the written report will be aligned.

The specific focus for the enquiry: It sounds obvious, but it is important to be very clear, from the outset of the report, about the specific focus for your enquiry, in order that the reader is able to understand, very quickly, the key issues that will be explored throughout the piece; as Taber (2013: 323) notes, 'writing up research is not like mystery writing, where the longer you keep the audience guessing, the better'. Remember that, while you are intimately connected to the study and immersed in both the experience and the evidence, the reader is unfamiliar with your enquiry and needs to get a very clear sense, from the first few paragraphs, of what it is all about.

The personal and professional rationale for the enquiry: You should aim to establish why this enquiry focus was important to you, in relation to your own identified development priorities at the outset of the project. You may make reference here to specific feedback that you received, prior to embarking on the project, which identified the focus as one of your areas for development, and how you came to decide that this particular area should form the focus for your enquiry. It can also be helpful to make reference to particular *Teachers' Standards* that are pertinent to your enquiry, as this also establishes professional importance.

The wider rationale and context: You should aim to make reference to appropriate research and/or relevant policy documents to support your rationale. This might be related to national policy developments or recent reports that help to demonstrate the significance of your chosen focus as an important area of practice for teachers. A detailed exploration of literature is not required at this stage, as that will be developed in the literature review, so confine yourself here to key documents that support the justification of your focus as important in having an impact on outcomes for learners.

The local context: You may wish to refer to local issues that informed your rationale. There may have been particular features of the teaching and learning context that influenced your choice of enquiry focus, such as the curriculum or assessment approaches of the school or setting in which the enquiry took place, or a teaching and learning issue being introduced or developed across the whole school. In providing information about the school or setting, be selective about the details you choose to provide, ensuring that they are directly relevant to your enquiry. Remember to attend to ethical considerations and maintain confidentiality even at this early stage in your account: do not provide so much detail about the location or nature of the school or setting that it could be identified from your description.

The objectives that guide the enquiry: It is very important to state the objectives for your enquiry, as these are essential to ensuring clarity of purpose and alignment throughout the study. The objectives are likely to be stated three times within the written report: here, in the introduction, to establish a clear focus for the enquiry; at the beginning of the enquiry design chapter to demonstrate how the enquiry plan was guided by and is appropriate to the objectives; and in the final, concluding chapter, to facilitate a clear review of findings in relation to the stated aims. The objectives stated in the introduction should be clear and relevant.

CASE STUDY 10.1

Fabiha, a School Direct PGCE primary student, wrote the following introduction to the written report of her action research enquiry.

Facilitating intellectual engagement within history lessons with Year 1 children: an action research enquiry

Griffith and Burns (2012: 2) consider engagement to be the core component required for a lesson to be effective. This intuitive deduction is supported by Berliner (1990: 3), who concludes that the more that children are engaged in a lesson the better their outcomes. With this in mind, the focus of this action research project is Teaching Standard 4.1: Imparting knowledge and skill through effective use of lesson time (DfE, 2011: 11).

The title and opening paragraph provide the reader with a clear understanding of the specific focus of the enquiry, with some reference to literature and the *Teachers' Standards* to support her professional rationale. This could potentially be further supported by considering the wider context, such as recognising the contested nature of 'engagement', with reference to appropriate research.

During my first placement I found it difficult to keep all children engaged in every lesson. Fear that the class had not fully understood my input led to an overemphasis on teacher-talk that resulted in some children becoming disengaged from their learning. As a consequence, the effective engagement of learners throughout lessons was identified as a focus for development.

(Continued)

This brief and honest paragraph sets out Fabiha's personal rationale for selecting this particular focus. Reference to some supporting evidence, such as feedback received on the previous placement, could strengthen this section further.

My final placement, and therefore this enquiry, was based in a Year 1 class who had recently switched from afternoons of child-initiated learning to more traditionally structured teacher-led lessons. At the start of this placement, I found it particularly difficult to keep children engaged during the afternoon lessons and many of the children were noticeably tired. History lessons were allocated to this time of the school day, so it seemed like a suitable subject within which to contextualise my enquiry.

This paragraph continues to identify the personal rationale for the enquiry focus and also clearly sets out the local context. Again, some reference to supporting evidence would be valuable, to convince the reader (or marker, for an assessed piece of work) that Fabiha has found it difficult to sustain children's engagement during the afternoon lessons.

I believe that every minute of time in the classroom can make a difference. As teachers, we have control over how our lesson time is used and should make every effort to use it to actively engage children in learning. However, the ways in which to engage children are infinite and for trainee teachers, in particular, it can be a daunting challenge. This enquiry is therefore a great opportunity to research, implement and evaluate current ideas around engaging children in their learning.

Fabiha has used this final paragraph to summarise this section as a whole, before moving on to state her enquiry objectives. She should seek to avoid including unsubstantiated claims, such as 'the ways in which to engage children are infinite', in order to ensure that her work has rigour and credibility.

In order to develop my practice within this standard I chose three enquiry objectives:

1. to develop knowledge and understanding of the key factors involved in effectively engaging children in their learning
2. to explore and analyse the impact of my lessons on children's engagement
3. to evaluate the effectiveness of my approaches to engaging children in their learning.

She concludes the introduction with some sound objectives that she used to guide the study. The second objective is a little unclear, as it suggests that she is looking for evidence of engagement rather than of learning. Remember that learning is the most significant measure of the effectiveness of your teaching. With this in mind, the second objective could perhaps be clarified: 'To analyse the impact of engaging the children in their learning'.

SETTING THE TONE AND STYLE FOR THE REPORT

The introduction does not just introduce the key issues for exploration throughout the enquiry. It also sets the tone for the report and, as such, must be attended to with care, appropriate academic rigour and criticality right from the start; as McNiff (2016b: 253) suggests, 'a readerly text says what it means to say, without ambiguity'. Remember that the reader may only read your account once (this is particularly true of an academic marker), so clarity of purpose from the outset is very important. When editing your introductory section, imagine you are reading it for the first time, with no prior knowledge of the study, and ask yourself whether, in that context, its purpose is crystal clear. Your aim is to reassure the reader that the whole piece is going to be a purposeful, intelligent and enjoyable read, so, in addition to writing with explicit criticality, it is necessary to establish a clear and concise writing style, with good academic practice from the outset.

HOW TO BE CRITICAL IN THE INTRODUCTION

The introduction is a short section of your written report and tends to deal with rather functional aspects of your research. As such, it can be easy to overlook the opportunities it presents to demonstrate your criticality.

Identify 'contested' issues: As a critical, intelligent writer, you should demonstrate your recognition of any 'contested' issues that are relevant to your study. For example, if your study focuses on facilitating children's use of success criteria to support the self-assessment of their work, you might, briefly, explore the potential downsides of using success criteria, such as the way in which children might use them as 'checklists' rather than as guides to support improvement in their work. In this way, you convince the reader that you do not uncritically accept elements of 'good practice' as 'always a good thing' and beyond challenge, like motherhood and apple pie.

CRITICAL TASK 10.1

In Table 10.1 we have identified three aspects of teachers' practice that might, with some focusing, form the basis for action research projects and, in the second column, suggested a 'motherhood and apple pie' view about why these elements of practice are 'obviously' good for children's learning. To complete the final column, identify ways in which the established or obvious view might be challenged, preferably with reference to published research or other literature. We'll give you our own suggestions towards the end of the chapter.

(Continued)

Table 10.1 Motherhood and apple pie views and contesting views

Element of practice	Motherhood and apple pie view	Contesting view
Modelling	Teachers should model how to do things so that children can learn skills from a 'more knowledgeable other'.	
Providing feedback	Teachers need to provide children with feedback to identify their mistakes and give them advice on how to make progress.	
Early years teacher talk	Teachers should join in with child-initiated play so that they can develop the children's vocabulary and challenge their thinking through questioning.	

Avoid unsubstantiated claims: You should aim to avoid the inclusion of any unsubstantiated claims in your introduction, as this would not be a good start. An unsubstantiated claim is a statement that is not supported with reference to evidence and this is an easy slip to make; surprisingly, such claims often feature in the opening sentence of reports, as in the following example:

> The role of assessment in teaching and learning has been the centre of debate over the last two decades.

This sounds impressive, but, as there is no reference to any evidence to support the statement, a reader is likely to ask how the writer knows this to be the case and an academic marker is likely to write 'How do you know?' in the margin of the text.

Explore the validity of key research: It is important to demonstrate your intelligent criticality, from the outset of your report, about claims or assertions from published research or other relevant sources; it is important to ask the 'How do you know?' question about other people's claims, just as much as about your own. This is also true if referring to national policy documents such as the National Curriculum, Ofsted reports or Department for Education guidelines, which are sometimes referred to in almost hallowed terms by student teachers, as though the National Curriculum should never be questioned or challenged.

Signpost to further criticality in your report: As the introduction is such a short section, it is not possible to go into great depth, so it can be a good idea to indicate here that you recognise that some issues require more critical engagement and signpost the reader to the sections of the report you will return to in order to consider them in more depth.

WRITING WITH CLARITY AND PURPOSE

When writing any section of your report, it is worth asking yourself, 'What am I trying to achieve in this section?'. Once you are clear about this, think carefully about the best order for all the key ideas or elements so that your work has a logical flow and is easy to follow. It can be very helpful to make your thinking about the structure explicit to the reader, so that they understand why you have chosen to guide them through the issues in a particular order: this is very reassuring for the reader, as they will understand that you have thought carefully about the shape and flow of the entire piece.

You should, of course, aim to ensure that there are no grammatical, punctuation or referencing errors in this first section of the report, so that the reader can settle into reading and enjoying your account without the distraction of unnecessary errors. We have included a number of helpful hints about academic writing in Chapter 15.

Finally, remember that some ethical issues are likely to arise in the introductory section and these should be tackled robustly to give the reader confidence that you understand the importance of ethics within your enquiry. The anonymity of the school, staff and children involved must be maintained throughout, so do not name the school, setting or specific class or classes: provide only general and relevant information about the school and age group of the children or young people involved. Similarly, it should be clearly established that your enquiry was focused firmly on the development of your own practice, and there should be no explicit or implied criticism of the school or colleagues within it.

RESPONSE TO CRITICAL TASK 10.1

In this task, we asked you to complete the final column of the table below by identifying ways in which the established or obvious view of the teacher's impact might be challenged, preferably with reference to published research or other literature.

Table 10.2   Response to motherhood and apple pie views and contesting views

Element of practice	Motherhood and apple pie view	Contesting view
Modelling	Teachers should model how to do things so that children can learn skills from a 'more knowledgeable other'.	The potential problem with modelling is that it stifles children's creativity, as they merely copy the model provided by the teacher. To combat this, Eperjesi (2020) suggests that, in art lessons, teachers would be best to model skills rather than products.
Providing feedback	Teachers need to provide children with feedback to identify their mistakes and give them advice on how to make progress.	Of course, feedback can be helpful. It can also be demotivating, and sometimes devastating, for children to have all their mistakes pointed out and be required to do 'corrections'. Middleton et al. (2020) suggest that learners' emotional responses are highly significant in relation to the impact of feedback on progress.
Early years teacher talk	Teachers should join in with child-initiated play so that they can develop the children's vocabulary and challenge their thinking through questioning.	Fisher (2016) gives several real examples of adults who, somewhat clumsily, try to join in with children's play and end up dominating the verbal exchanges, disrupting the children's rich and valuable independent or collaborative learning.

SUMMARY FOR THIS CHAPTER

In this chapter, we have begun to explore the nature of an effective written report for your action research enquiry through identifying the key features that should be included in your introduction, related to the focus, the rationale, the context and the objectives. We have also considered the importance of setting the tone for the report through writing critically, concisely and academically from the start and, as a result, reassuring the reader that they are going to enjoy engaging with a well-considered and intelligent piece of work. In the following chapter, we will explore how to make the most of your critical engagement with reading through writing an effective literature review.

Do:

- be clear about the focus for the enquiry
- explain the personal and professional rationale for the enquiry
- demonstrate how this relates to both the local and wider contexts
- share the enquiry objectives that guide the study
- establish a purposeful, critical and concise tone for the written report.

Don't:

- make unsubstantiated claims
- forget to maintain the highest ethical standards, including anonymity of participants
- make unnecessary errors in punctuation, grammar or referencing.

FURTHER READING

The following sources may also support you in considering how to create a strong opening to your action research report:

McConville-Rae, D. (2015) 'The effect of higher-order questioning on pupil understanding, as assessed using mind maps and the solo taxonomy', *The STeP Journal*, 2 (2): 5–18.

This article is written by a student teacher reflecting on a professional enquiry undertaken as part of their initial teacher education, in which they provide a good, professional rationale for their chosen focus, both in relation to evidence about good practice and their own development priorities.

McNiff, J. (2016) *Writing Up Your Action Research Project*. Abingdon: Routledge.

Written by one of the best-known authors in the field of action research, this book provides valuable and clear guidance about the writing process in education action research.

Murray, C. (2015) 'To what extent does philosophy with children promote the discussion of political philosophical themes?', *The STeP Journal*, 2 (3): 18–30.

This interesting article, written by a student teacher, places the rationale for the study in a wider context, drawing on current events of national importance to inform the identification of a focus for the study.

11

WRITING THE LITERATURE REVIEW

OBJECTIVES FOR THIS CHAPTER

- To explore the purpose of a literature review
- To explore what kind of literature to review and how to review it
- To explore the difference between a literature review and a good literature review.

THE PURPOSE OF A LITERATURE REVIEW

In this chapter, we will consider the purpose of a literature review, as part of writing up your action research project. Links will be made back to Chapter 4, in which we considered how to select literature sources and how to read critically. We will now consider how to review the literature in a critical manner and how you might structure this section of your account. Some examples will be included to support you in identifying what makes a 'good' literature review, as well as exploring some common pitfalls and how to avoid them.

IDENTIFYING THE FEATURES OF EFFECTIVE PRACTICE

As discussed in Chapter 4, engaging with relevant literature should help you to identify the features of effective practice in relation to your focus and support you in developing your knowledge and understanding of these features, thus enabling you to make informed decisions about how to develop your practice as you undertake the research. The literature review allows you to demonstrate your own knowledge and understanding explicitly to the reader, as you explore the current state of knowledge that has already been established in relation to your chosen focus. When you write up the implementation section of your assignment or dissertation (see Chapter 13), you will make links back to the literature explored within the literature review to demonstrate how it informed your developing practice, as you undertook the research.

One of the most common difficulties experienced by new teachers in writing the literature review is remembering the need to remain focused on practice, rather than on theory, policy or the history of education. While some justification of your selection of focus is needed, this can be achieved within the context and rationale section of the introduction (see Chapter 10) or, briefly, at the beginning of the literature review, with the remainder of the review focusing on practice. For example, if the focus of your enquiry is making effective use of talk partners to support children's learning in science, most of your literature review should focus on the key factors that can impact on the effectiveness of the talk partner approach, such as how children are paired, the time allocated for talk partner discussion, modelling how to be a 'good' talk partner and, most importantly, how to facilitate effective talk, rather than using the literature review to try to convince the reader that talk partners are a useful approach. If too much time is spent on seeking to justify your selection of focus, it becomes difficult for you to demonstrate, within the literature review, that you know and understand the key factors that will inform your practice and help improve your teaching. Your implementation section (see Chapter 13) will be firmly focused on your own practice, so it will be difficult to make links back to the literature review if that is not also primarily focused on practice.

This leads on to the question of when the literature review should be written. Punch (2009: 103) suggests that many graduates consider writing the literature review to be a 'daunting' task. Some suggest writing it at the point of undertaking most of the reading (before undertaking the enquiry), so that they have already completed one section of the written report in advance of starting the research. While there are some potential benefits to such an approach, such as minimising the risk of 'losing' any literature sources between reading and writing, this can be problematic, not least in terms of deciding what to include and what to leave out.

Whatever your reasons for writing up your enquiry, it is likely that you will have a word limit for the piece as a whole and you may even have a suggested word limit for each section. If, as encouraged in Chapter 4, you have read as widely as possible, there is every chance that you will find it challenging to stick within the word limit for the literature review (note: this does not mean that you should engage in less reading). As well as writing concisely, you will therefore need to be very selective about what you include; as Taber (2013) identifies, unless working at doctoral level, there is no expectation that you will have read *all* of the relevant literature and your literature review will reflect that. You should consider 'quality over quantity', by which we mean that you should engage deeply with a smaller number of sources, rather than engaging superficially with as many sources as possible just to show how much you have read; of course, those sources need to be carefully selected and you will need to achieve some balance, so that you are not over-reliant on a very small number of sources.

As has been established, the emphasis should be on exploring the key factors of effective practice relating to your focus and, in Chapter 4, we suggested the use of a mind map or other visual representation to capture these key factors as you are reading. However, you may find that exploring all of these key factors within your literature review is still too much, no matter how succinct your writing style. You should therefore place far more emphasis on those key factors which are most pertinent to your own enquiry; returning to the example given earlier in this chapter, if the key factor of modelling how to be a 'good' talk partner was not explored during your own enquiry (perhaps because the children already understood this or perhaps because the research period ended before you had a chance to explore this), then it does not need to be emphasised within the literature review, as you will not be referring back to it in the implementation section of your written account. Thus, as Silverman (2017) advises, there are some benefits to writing the literature review after undertaking the research, so that the relevant key factors can be followed like 'threads' throughout the written account as a whole.

IDENTIFYING THE FEATURES OF CHILDREN'S PROGRESS

It may also be beneficial to use literature to explore the features of children's expected progress, so that you can identify the impact your practice is having. For example, if your chosen focus is to improve your use of modelling in mathematics, with the intention that it will have a positive impact on the development of children's mathematical reasoning skills, then, as well as exploring the features of effective modelling within your literature review, you may also find it helpful to consider what the literature has to say about what progress in children's mathematical reasoning skills 'looks like'. Not only will this help you to identify it, it will also enable you to support the claims that you make about children's progress in your implementation section (see Chapter 13), particularly if you use the literature to develop a critical framework, as discussed below.

CREATING A CRITICAL FRAMEWORK

As mentioned in Chapter 4, as well as using literature to inform the development of your own knowledge and understanding, you can also draw on it to synthesise a framework of criteria by which to judge the quality and development of your practice and to judge the impact of your practice on children's learning. Your framework should be as specific as possible; writing in vague terms will not help you to make judgements, nor will it help you to communicate your understanding to the reader. It is often best to present this framework at the end of the literature review, as it requires you to draw upon the exploration of literature which precedes it. Presenting it as a series of bullet points is often a clear and efficient way of communicating the framework that you have developed.

PLANNING A STRUCTURE FOR THE LITERATURE REVIEW

Given the need to remain focused and to utilise the word count to maximum effect, planning a structure for your literature review is crucial, in order to ensure that it fulfils its purpose, as discussed above. Time spent at the planning stage will save time during the writing stage, as well as assisting you in producing a coherent written account, with clear links between the sections. You will need to return to your mind map (or other notes) created at the point of reading and compare this with the evidence gathered during the research phase; consider which of the key factors relating to your focus, identified through your engagement with the literature, were relevant to your own research and which were not. (You may find it helpful to use colour coding to match key issues within the evidence to the relevant sections of your mind map.) Consider also whether any additional key factors relating to your focus emerged during the course of your enquiry, which you had not previously identified through your reading; this might suggest that you need to revisit the literature and read more specifically before continuing.

Remember that the key factors you explored during the enquiry itself should be the ones emphasised in the literature review, so that it connects with the implementation and with the conclusions you draw in the review of findings and method (explored further in Chapter 14). As with all sections of your written report, you should aim to provide a clear introduction to the literature review section, outlining its purpose and the main points that you intend to explore, as well as their relevance.

CASE STUDY 11.1

Here is an example of how Sian, a PGCE primary student, structured her literature review.
    Sian began with an opening paragraph which briefly defined questioning (her selected focus) and touched upon the potential value of using questioning effectively. As she had also considered the potential value of questioning in the context and rationale section of her assignment, this was perfectly appropriate.

Much research has been carried out on the topic of questioning. The consensus is that when integrated into classroom practice, it can be implemented in various positive ways: to check understanding, elicit pupils' misconceptions, 'recall facts . . . and maintain control'. Questions are also often used to 'stimulate interest and curiosity

(Continued)

in a topic' (Almeida 2010: 306). Before further considering literature on this subject, it is important to define the concept. Cotton (2001: 1) states that a question is 'any sentence which has an interrogative form or function'. These often require 'information seeking' and usually 'stimulate some kind of mental activity or thinking' (Wilen, 1991: 6).

She then explored the following key factors: pre-planning the questions to be asked, including how these might be sequenced; closed versus open questions; questions requiring low-level responses versus those requiring higher-level responses; 'wait-time' and 'think time'; and talk partner discussion before answering questions.

There may be some other key issues that could be relevant to effective questioning, such as the challenge of pupils who never volunteer to answer or how to respond to incorrect answers. While these are relevant to the overall topic of effective questioning (and were indeed identified on her mind map), Sian had not explored these issues in her own enquiry, so did not intend to explore them in her implementation section, as she had no evidence upon which to base any such discussion. To demonstrate that she knew and understood that other factors can impact on effective questioning, Sian concluded her literature review with the following sentence as part of her final paragraph:

However, I am aware that questioning is an extremely broad and widely researched topic and that I have only examined a relatively small portion of this for the purposes of this project.

Different views exist as to whether subheadings should be used or not, but you may find it helpful to do so in order to keep the literature review focused and appropriately structured. While Sian *concluded* her literature review by acknowledging that she had not explored all aspects of questioning, you may prefer to do this *before* exploring the relevant key issues, e.g. 'There are many factors involved in effective questioning, such as . . . However, as this is a small scale enquiry, conducted over a relatively short period of time, I have chosen to focus on the factors most pertinent to my own practice'. Feedback on Sian's assignment noted that 'There are very clear links between the implementation and the literature review, demonstrating your ability to connect research and practice'.

Taking an approach such as the one in Case study 11.1, where the literature review is structured around the relevant key issues relating to the topic, can be an important first step in seeking to avoid another common difficulty: that is, simply presenting or describing what has been read. This tends to be compounded when the writer seeks to present their reading as a chronological journey, for example, 'Firstly I read . . ., who stated that . . . I then read . . . who suggested . . .'. This overly descriptive approach is not only rather dull for the reader, but it also prevents you from demonstrating your skills in thinking and writing critically, which will be explored in more depth below.

CRITICAL TASK 11.1

Remember Anna from Chapter 4, the primary teacher trainee on a School Direct salaried route, who was seeking to develop her approach to guiding pupils' self-reflection? Anna has now undertaken lots of reading in relation to her focus and has some spare time available before she embarks upon her research. She is considering writing her literature review but has been advised that it would be better to wait until she has undertaken the research. What would you advise her to do at this point which will put her in a good position when she comes to write the literature review at a later date?

HOW TO BE 'CRITICAL' IN YOUR REVIEW OF THE LITERATURE

In Chapter 4 we considered the importance of reading critically, rather than taking everything at face value. We explored, through a series of questions, some of the factors to consider when engaging with the literature and these are equally relevant when writing up the literature review, to demonstrate your critical thinking skills to the reader; if you have thought about it, you need to write about it, as you need to go beyond simply summarising what you have read, as advised by Koshy (2010). For example, if you noted during your reading that a particular piece of research was overly reliant on a particular type of evidence, then communicate this to the reader, for example 'From her research, Author A (2015) noted that . . . However, it is worth noting that the only evidence presented consisted of her own field notes and I therefore have reservations about the validity of her research, as triangulation has not been achieved'.

The questions, from Chapter 4, to support you in reading critically are presented below. Remember that 'advice' and research findings need to be handled differently and therefore the questions that you ask will differ, depending on the literature source.

If the source is 'advice':

- Who is the author and what qualifies them to be giving advice?
- When was this published and where was this published?
- Is the author drawing upon the work of others, whether that is also advice or whether it is research?
- How does the advice given compare with what you have read in other sources?

If the source is research, some of the above questions will still be relevant, as well as the questions below:

- What was the nature and focus of the research and how closely does this align with your own focus?

- How reliable is the research?
- How valid is the research?
- Was the research conducted ethically?
- How does it compare to your experience?

Now that you are writing your literature review, you need to comment on some of these considerations, as well as addressing them at the point of reading; the person reading your written account will not know that you can read critically, unless you explicitly communicate this to them. However, if you have a word limit, you will not be able to comment on all aspects for every piece. The decisions that you make (about which aspects of which pieces to comment upon) will further demonstrate your ability to be critical to the reader. Try to avoid over-simplifying. For example, a comment such as 'As Author X was once a teacher, I feel that I am able to trust their advice' does little to demonstrate your critical thinking. Try to delve more deeply than this, by really engaging with the research and getting stuck into it. How did Author A come up with their advice? Was it research-informed or does it align with current research? Then consider the quality of the research, by engaging with the questions outlined above.

CRITICAL TASK 11.2

Below are a couple of excerpts from assignment/dissertation literature reviews:

> Student teacher Alex writes: 'Children need to be able to work together collaboratively in order to develop their own opinions (Eperjesi and Wire, 2020).'

> Student teacher Bethany writes: 'Daines (1986, cited in Way, 2011) states that research shows that 93% of questions used in a classroom environment are questions that lead to lower order thinking, concentrating on recalling facts'.

Both student teachers appear to accept these statements at face value and move on to new points immediately. What would you suggest they should be considering, then commenting upon, within their literature reviews, in order to demonstrate that they can read, think and write critically?

As well as considering what is said within the literature, it is important to also consider what has been omitted, as this may be even more significant. For example, Helen, a BEd primary student, considers research carried out in relation to the effective use of talk partners in the literature review of her dissertation. She identifies some similarities and differences between the research and her own enquiry. She notes that the research findings indicate that the use of talk partners seemed to lead to visibly increased amounts of work from the children, but also notes that there is no evidence that the work produced was of good quality or met the success criteria. This is significant, as it may raise questions about the validity of the study.

So far in this section, we have considered how to be 'critical' in relation to individual sources, but the way in which you construct your review also provides opportunity to demonstrate your criticality. Earlier on in this chapter we discussed structuring your literature review around the relevant key issues, possibly making use of subheadings to create subsections. Within each subsection, you should aim to take a skilful approach to 'weaving' your discussion about the different sources together. Try to:

Compare sources: Consider the similarities between sources. While you may have reservations about the validity or reliability of a particular piece of research, you may be reassured if the findings are mirrored by other, similar studies.

Contrast sources: Consider the differences between sources. Consider why the differences might exist. For example, is one source opinion-based, written by an author whose experiences of teaching were in higher education 30 years ago, while another is based on robust and recent research, in a range of primary schools across England and Wales? Note that the potential reasons for differences are rarely as obvious as the example given here, so you will need to reflect critically and be suitably tentative when exploring this in writing.

Connect sources: This goes beyond comparing and contrasting. Consider whether there are any less obvious links between sources and key issues, which may well mean making connections between different subsections of your literature review. For example, when exploring the importance of allocating sufficient time for children to engage in talk partner discussion, you may make connections with your discussion about how children are paired, as children who have been paired effectively are more likely to remain on task and therefore waste less time. Again, this reiterates the value of writing your literature review after undertaking the research, as these connections are likely to become more obvious to you once you have 'lived' them.

Comment: Make links to your own previous experiences, both as a teacher and as a learner. Consider how what you have explored compares to what you have experienced, particularly where you have identified differences between sources. You will obviously do far more of this when you write the implementation section of your written account, as you will be presenting the findings of your own enquiry and comparing these to the literature, but you are not a 'blank slate' at the point of writing the literature review, so including occasional opinions and experiences can be very valuable in further establishing the context of your enquiry.

While you may refer to literature in all sections of your written report, this will be most extensive in your literature review and it is important to consider the use of direct quotes and paraphrase and the balance of these. Within the text, direct quotes are usually placed within quotation marks (or indented for longer direct quotes). Wyse (2012: 64) suggests that 'the best academic writing uses quotations sparingly'. Overuse of quotations can impact negatively on the flow of your writing and may also suggest a lack of understanding; if you are able to paraphrase effectively, this is likely to convince the reader that you do understand what you have read. You may choose to use a direct quote when it makes a point very clearly or when it provides an opportunity to demonstrate your criticality, but you must ensure that you integrate the quote into your discussion rather than inserting it as a 'stand-alone'; it should support your discussion, rather than 'being' the discussion.

RESPONSE TO CRITICAL TASK 11.1

Anna has undertaken lots of reading, relating to her focus, and has some time available which she would like to use productively. However, she has been advised not to write her literature review until after she has undertaken the enquiry. She needed some advice about how to use her time.

It is excellent that Anna has some time available and is keen to use it to 'get ahead' with her literature review, but writing it before undertaking the research could mean that she does not focus on the key issues most pertinent to her own enquiry. There are lots of useful things that she could do now, that will help her when she does come to write the literature review, such as expanding her literature search to read more widely (while remaining focused); creating a mind map of the key issues; colour coding these on the mind map to match the literature sources (she could use highlighter pens for articles she has printed, the highlighter tool on electronic texts and sticky tabs on books); compiling a draft reference list which can be edited later. The final point will certainly save time later, as it is a time-consuming task, but it is important to complete it correctly; additionally, compiling it at this point may help Anna to identify possible 'gaps' in her literature, such as over-reliance on certain sources, lack of research journal articles or lack of recent sources.

RESPONSE TO CRITICAL TASK 11.2

Student teacher Alex writes: 'Children need to be able to work together collaboratively in order to develop their own opinions (Eperjesi and Wire, 2020).'

Student teacher Bethany writes: 'Daines (1986, cited in Way, 2011) states that research shows that 93% of questions used in a classroom environment are questions that lead to lower order thinking, concentrating on recalling facts'.

We asked you to suggest what these student teachers should be considering, then commenting upon, within their literature reviews, in order to demonstrate that they can read, think and write critically. Here is the feedback that we would offer to these two student teachers:

Student teacher Alex: That is quite a powerful statement. You might consider what qualifies Eperjesi and Wire to make such a statement. You might consider whether this is Eperjesi and Wire's opinion (and if so, what is it based upon?) or whether it is based on research. If the latter, you might consider the validity and reliability of the research: is the claim reasonable? You might consider how this compares to your own experience.

Student teacher Bethany: You might consider whether Daines undertook the research or whether he is commenting upon research undertaken by someone else. If the latter, you might explore whether Daines has interpreted the findings appropriately (this might require you to locate and engage with the original research). You might consider the validity and reliability of the research, the date of Daines' statement and whether it is relevant today (35 years later), and what the phrasing 'classroom environment' really means, seeking to clarify what age group was involved in the research and how relatable this is to your own enquiry.

SUMMARY FOR THIS CHAPTER

In this chapter, we have considered the purpose of the literature review. It is important to understand and acknowledge this, so that you can seek to avoid some of the potential pitfalls presented above. The literature review provides the opportunity to demonstrate your ability to handle the literature critically, as well as to establish the 'threads' that will run through the remainder of your written account. We have considered planning and structuring the literature review and emphasised the importance of focusing on practice. We have revisited the points to consider when reading critically, as outlined in Chapter 4, and explored how these might be applied to writing the literature review. In the next chapter, we will discuss how to write the enquiry design section of your written account.

Do:

- summarise the state of knowledge about the aspect of practice you are focusing on
- stay focused on effective practice
- engage critically with the literature through comparing sources and identifying strengths and limitations to studies
- create a critical framework by which to judge your developing practice and the impact it has on children's progress
- organise your literature review in a logical manner.

Don't:

- forget to review some literature in your literature review
- get sidetracked on policy, theory or the history of education
- simply present what you have read; you need to reflect and comment upon it in a critical manner.

FURTHER READING

The following texts may also support you in writing your literature review:

Byrom, T. (2016) 'Constructing the literature section', in I. Palaiologou, D. Needham and
    T. Male (eds), *Doing Research in Education: Theory and Practice*. London: Sage, pp. 118–35.

This chapter offers an accessible discussion of both engaging with the literature (and may
therefore also support you in relation to Chapter 4 of this book) and writing the literature
review of your written account; it includes some useful case studies and concludes with
some 'key points to remember'.

Hart, C. (2018) *Doing a Literature Review: Releasing the Research Imagination*. 2nd edn.
    London: Sage.

This text provides a comprehensive guide to all stages of completing a literature review,
from beginning to search for relevant literature sources to writing up the review in your
written account. It is important to remember that the text is not specific to education and
was originally written for people working at master's and doctoral level.

Walliman, N. (2020) *Your Research Project: Designing, Planning and Getting Started*. 4th edn.
    London: Sage.

Chapter 5 of Walliman's text focuses on all stages of the literature review, with some particularly useful advice on how to read, and incorporate your reading, critically. However,
it is important to note that this text is not specific to education, or to action research.

12

WRITING THE ENQUIRY DESIGN OR RESEARCH PLAN

OBJECTIVES FOR THIS CHAPTER

- To explore the purpose of the enquiry design or research plan section of the report
- To explain what to put in and what to leave out
- To explain the difference between a method and a methodology
- To establish the importance for a researcher to 'position' themselves in relation to research paradigms and methodology.

PURPOSE OF THE ENQUIRY DESIGN OR RESEARCH PLAN

In this chapter, we will explore how to write a really good 'enquiry design' section or chapter in the written report of your action research study. This section or chapter might, variously, be called 'research plan', 'research design', 'enquiry plan' or even 'methodology'; these are all similar things but we will use the term 'enquiry design' throughout this chapter.

Bassey (1995: 16) states that 'researchers are expected to be truthful in data collection, analysis and the reporting of findings'. There is an ethical need for all studies to be transparent about the methods adopted and the care that the researcher(s) took to ensure that these methods addressed the intended purpose and stated objectives of the project. The purpose of the enquiry design is to set out, clearly, the plans that you had for your action research enquiry, how you ensured that these were as rigorous and purposeful as possible, and how you planned to make sense of your evidence and make use of it in the evaluation of your practice. It is also important to demonstrate, in this section, how you addressed all ethical concerns related to undertaking a school-based enquiry. This is a lot to ask of a section that is often relatively short, so it is important to be focused and selective about what to include.

It is valuable to inform your enquiry design with reference to appropriate literature about education research and practitioner or action research, as this enables you to be clear about the nature and purpose of your enquiry and this supports reflection on the strengths and limitations of your chosen methods. This kind of reading will also enable you to explore a number of concepts that we explored briefly in Chapter 1 that may be unfamiliar, such as research 'paradigms', and will enable you, in the writing of your enquiry design section, to 'position' yourself in relation to the broader paradigm within which action research is located. Remember that research comes in many forms, from scientific and clinical studies within the *positivist* paradigm, to action research, which is located within the *interpretivist* paradigm. A positivist approach is likely to draw on quantitative data from large samples to draw conclusions in an objective and reliable way, whereas an interpretivist approach deals more with the subjectivity of the social world and tends to draw on qualitative data to seek a meaningful and valid insight into the complex realities of aspects of daily life. The life of a school or other educational setting is full of complexities, and teaching and learning is a hugely complex interaction and interplay between countless human factors, which cannot be readily measured but which the action researcher aims to understand.

Wider reading may also support understanding of other subtleties in education research, such as the difference between a method and a methodology. Action research is a methodology, an overarching framework that guides an individual's enquiry and provides a way of thinking about understanding their practice. A method is a particular approach to gathering evidence, such as observation of children's responses or scrutinising children's written work, that is selected by an individual researcher to enable them to address their stated objectives.

Holliday (2016: 46) emphasises the need for researchers to 'show their workings', being clear about how they managed the process of their enquiry and its tensions. The enquiry design section or chapter should enable you to demonstrate that, throughout your project, you had a sound understanding of the nature of action research, a clear focus for your action research enquiry, a clear plan for gathering relevant and appropriate evidence and for addressing all ethical considerations. The aspect of this chapter or section that is often overlooked is the need to be clear about how you planned to analyse your evidence. In order to be analytical about your evidence, it is important to communicate clearly what you planned to look for in your data and the criteria that you planned to use to make judgements, both about the children's learning and the quality of your teaching. It can be very valuable here to draw on ideas from your literature review to establish a framework by which you intended to make these judgements. For example, you may have identified a useful starting point for analysing the quality of your questioning, which could be adapted to create your own criteria by which to judge how your questioning skills progressed, such as the table suggested by Wragg and Brown (2001), which might help you categorise your questions in relation to whether they are clear or confused, encouraging or threatening, and whether they encourage recall or observation.

Another purpose of the enquiry design chapter or section is to indicate that you planned a cyclical approach to the improvement of your practice, based on analysis and evaluation. Some student teachers include a diagram drawn from a book or website to show their understanding of the spiralling and developmental nature of action research, and it might be valuable to create a diagrammatic representation of your enquiry plan, indicating your own starting points, the evidence you planned to gather, what you planned to look for in your evidence and how you planned to evaluate your practice. Summarising your plan in this way might be helpful, at least for the first research cycle.

Finally, your enquiry design should show how you addressed all the ethical considerations that we explored in Chapter 5 and Chapter 7. There are some ethical issues that every student teacher undertaking an action research project will need to consider (e.g. confidentiality and anonymity), but you should also take care here to explain any subtle ethical challenges that you faced and how you addressed these (e.g. ensuring that your data collection did not impact negatively on children's learning).

STRUCTURE OF THE ENQUIRY DESIGN SECTION OR CHAPTER

The enquiry design section or chapter normally starts with a restatement of the enquiry or research objectives or questions; these are the guiding questions or statements that remind you, throughout the process, what you would need to find out in order to understand the detail of your practice and its impact on the learners you were working with during the project. The objectives should be phrased exactly as they are in the introductory chapter or section of your report. It is valuable to restate your objectives here, at the outset of your enquiry design section, as these should be absolutely central to how you developed your plans, and there should be an obvious alignment between the stated objectives, the evidence that you planned to gather and what you planned to look for in the evidence.

It is important to explain, even briefly, your research 'position'. This would normally include providing a clear explanation of your understanding of the nature of action research, with reference to appropriate literature, and why this methodology was appropriate for you to employ for this study; it may be worth taking a few words to explain the research paradigm that this relates to.

The most important aspect of this section or chapter is for you to explain and justify the methods you planned to adopt for collecting a range of meaningful and relevant data that enabled you to clearly address the stated objectives. You should aim to be explicit and specific about how you planned to gather each kind of evidence; this is especially true if you plan to report, in your findings and analysis section, on words that children have spoken. You can only present these in the form of a transcript if they represent a verbatim account (that is, if you audio-recorded them), so it is necessary to be clear in your plan as to how the words you report were 'captured'. Throughout, you should aim to justify your planned approaches to gathering data; reference to appropriate literature will support this justification and will also support you in exploring the potential limitations associated with your planned approaches and how you might address such challenges.

You should aim to explain how you planned to analyse your evidence or, to think of this in another way, be clear about what you planned to look for in your evidence. This should clearly relate to the stated objectives for the study. It is easy to assume that this is obvious from the context, but it is important to be explicit about this.

You should also demonstrate how you planned to make use of triangulation to increase the validity of your enquiry. Triangulation is sometimes thought of as collecting evidence from more than one source to shed light on an issue from more than one angle. While this is an essential part of developing a well-triangulated study, it is only part of the story, as triangulation only becomes triangulation when the various sources of evidence are drawn together in detailed analysis, as it is the analysis that enables the researcher to build a robust understanding of a complex situation. As we will explore further in the next chapter, this requires the action researcher to weave together evidence from a variety of sources in a coherent account, and, in doing so, this increases the validity of the enquiry.

Remember that 'validity' and 'reliability' have distinct meanings in research and should not be used interchangeably: validity refers to how well the evidence gathered and the analysis undertaken match the stated objectives of the research, whereas reliability refers to the extent to which a study can be said to be 'reproducible', which normally relates to the size of the sample, which, in education research, relates to the number of schools or children/young people involved in the study. (Refer to Chapter 6 for a more detailed discussion of the difference between validity and reliability.) Your enquiry design chapter should include an explanation of how you planned to increase validity through explicit triangulation of evidence and should also include a statement about the extent to which your evidence is reliable. If you have undertaken a small-scale study, it would usually be deemed to have low reliability; this should not be seen as a problem but should be acknowledged in your report.

At some stage in the enquiry design section or chapter, normally towards the end but sometimes nearer the beginning, it is important to be explicit about how you addressed the ethical considerations we discussed in Chapters 5 and 7, such as ethical gatekeeping, informed consent, confidentiality, and how you responded to any particular issues that arose in relation to your particular context, perhaps in relation to safeguarding vulnerable children or attending to school guidelines or policies.

While some sections of the enquiry plan should outline what you *planned* to do, in this section you should be explicit about the actions you took to ensure your study was ethically sound. For example, the reader does not need to know if you *planned* to ask senior staff within your school (the ethical gatekeepers) for their consent for you to undertake the enquiry; they need to be reassured that you *did so*. They don't need to know that you *planned* to engage with parents in relation to the enquiry; they need to be reassured that you did this in an appropriate manner, so your approach should be explained and a copy of any letter sent to parents should be appended. In the case of any letter or other pertinent documents in your appendices, remember that, in order to ensure anonymity, these may need to include some redaction to remove the school name and address.

CRITICAL TASK 12.1

Remember Jane, the School Direct PGCE primary student who was focusing on her developing use of differentiation? Here is a section from her enquiry design section. She decided against using a focus group, preferring to gain access to a wide range of evidence related to the learning of all children in the class.

> To undertake my action research project, I planned to work with all thirty children in the class to be able to gather evidence to provide me with insights into their learning and responses. Working with the whole class each week would enable me to collate the necessary quantitative and qualitative data to triangulate.

This is the end of Jane's section about gathering evidence and leaves the reader with some unanswered questions. What else should she include in this section?

CRITICAL TASK 12.2

Julie, a BEd primary student teacher, identifies, in her literature review, a way of thinking about questions that might form the basis for a useful framework for judging the effectiveness of her own questions:

> Wiggins and Wilbur (2015) discuss the features of 'good questions'. They state that 'good questions' stimulate ongoing thinking and enquiry, have multiple plausible answers, raise further questions, spark discussion and debate as well as demand evidence and reasoning because multiple answers exist.

How might she make use of this in the writing of her enquiry design?

COMMON OR POSSIBLE PITFALLS TO AVOID WHEN WRITING THE ENQUIRY DESIGN

Over the years of marking reports of action research enquiries, we have noticed several pitfalls that you should aim to avoid.

Avoid writing in general terms about enquiry plans: Having undertaken wide reading into research methods, it is possible for a student teacher writing their report to describe in broad terms their planned approach for gathering evidence, and even to demonstrate their good understanding of the strengths and limitations of certain methods, such as observation, field notes or audio-recording, without ever being specific about what it is that they planned to observe, make notes about or audio-record, or what specific insights it was hoped that these would provide. The main purpose of this section of the written report is for you to set out, as clearly and openly as possible, the data that you planned to gather and what you planned to look for within the data.

Avoid writing about approaches you did not plan to use: This is an interesting error that crops up from time to time, in which a student teacher writes in detail about the benefits and limitations of using a particular research method, only then to state that they did not use that as an approach to gathering data in their enquiry. There is not much point in using many words to explain the benefits and limitations of using interviews as part of an action research study if you did not actually use interviews as part of *your* study.

Avoid writing in great detail about ontology, epistemology, paradigms and such: In general, student teachers undertaking action research enquiries do not need to use many words explaining their ontological beliefs or epistemological position. This is partly because of the restricted word limit and partly because of the level of study: should you choose to complete a master's or doctoral degree, these issues will become increasingly important. Of course, it is particularly important not to get bogged down with these terms if you are not entirely sure that you understand them.

Avoid writing about validity and triangulation in isolation: While it is a good idea to demonstrate a sound grasp of these concepts, you should do so through discussing their application to your own enquiry. You should show how you decided on the evidence that you planned to gather, in order to ensure the validity of your enquiry, and how you planned to analyse this evidence in a triangulated way.

SOME GUIDANCE ON WHICH TENSE TO USE IN YOUR ENQUIRY DESIGN

An issue that is often somewhat flummoxing in the writing of the enquiry design section or chapter relates to the consistent use of tense. This is a result of the tension between the need to write a 'plan' for the enquiry, which sounds as though you should write about what you are going to do in the future, and the fact that, by the time you come to write the final draft of the plan in the assignment, you have already carried out the plan. In general, it is best to write your assignment as a retrospective account, as you are reporting on a project that has been undertaken, so in the enquiry design section you might make use of a forward-looking past tense, for example: 'At the outset of this project, I planned to . . .'. This enables you to be consistent in writing in the past tense, while also being clear that you had a plan that was in place before embarking on your enquiry. The exception to this would be when describing the ethical steps taken, which should be described in a straightforward past tense.

RESPONSE TO CRITICAL TASK 12.1

We asked what else Jane should include in this section of her enquiry design.

> To undertake my action research project, I planned to work with all thirty children in the class to be able to gather evidence to provide me with insights into their learning and responses. Working with the whole class each week would enable me to collate the necessary quantitative and qualitative data to triangulate.

When writing this, it was probably completely clear in Jane's head what the data was that she needed to gather in order to address her stated objectives. However, the reader is left wondering what specific kinds of 'quantitative and qualitative' data she planned to gather and how she planned to do so. Perhaps more importantly, Jane has not made clear what it was that she hoped the data would reveal or the insights that she would be searching for within the data. Being explicit and clear about all this would not just be beneficial to the reader, but also to Jane when she came to analyse her evidence.

RESPONSE TO CRITICAL TASK 12.2

We asked how Julie might make use of this section from her literature review in the writing of her enquiry design.

> Wiggins and Wilbur (2015) discuss the features of 'good questions'. They state that 'good questions' stimulate ongoing thinking and enquiry, have multiple plausible answers, raise further questions, spark discussion and debate as well as demand evidence and reasoning because multiple answers exist.

Julie has done a great job of identifying, in her literature review, a source that gives some specific criteria by which to judge whether a question is a 'good one'. Ultimately, the quality of her questions can only be judged through the quality of the responses from the learners, so this source reminds her that it is most important that she gathers good evidence of the children's answers, either through audio-recordings or detailed notes; the framework she has identified then provides a way for her to analyse these responses and evaluate the quality of her questions.

SUMMARY FOR THIS CHAPTER

In this chapter, we have considered the elements that make a clear and convincing enquiry design section or chapter in your action research report. This should begin with a restatement of your enquiry objectives, which should help to demonstrate the clear alignment between what you were trying to find out and the data that you gathered, the details of which should be clearly explained. You should aim to define what you planned to look for in your data and to establish a clear framework for how you intended to judge the effectiveness or impact of your practice. The chapter should include a well-considered section relating to steps you took to ensure your study was ethically sound.

In the following chapter, we will explore how to write a really good 'implementation and analysis' section. This is the heart of the written report so the most important and, in many ways, the most exciting part, as it is the presentation of your own research.

Do:

- restate your objectives
- explain why action research was an appropriate methodology for your enquiry
- be clear about your planned methods, in relation to both gathering and analysing data
- include your own evaluations as a valuable source of evidence
- draw on pertinent sources from your literature review to support the creation of criteria by which to judge the effectiveness of your developing practice
- be clear about how you addressed ethical issues
- refer to appropriate literature about educational research
- be critical about your own chosen methods.

Don't:

- write in general terms about data
- write about data that you did not gather
- use long words such as 'epistemology' if you are not completely sure what they mean
- get confused about which tense you are writing in.

FURTHER READING

The following sources may also support you in writing a clear and concise enquiry design:

Bassey, M. (1995) *Creating Education through Research: A Global Perspective of Educational Research for the 21st Century*. Newark: Kirklington Moor Press and Edinburgh: British Educational Research Association.

This very accessible book provides clear and valuable insight into the need for clarity and openness in communicating about research and enquiry design.

Thomas, G. (2017) *How to Do Your Research Project: A Guide for Students.* 3rd edn. London: Sage.

Chapter 5 of this clear and accessible book includes a very helpful section on research paradigms.

Wragg, E. (2012) *An Introduction to Classroom Observation.* Classic edn. Abingdon: Routledge.

This book provides some frameworks for taking a structured approach to making valuable observations in educational settings.

13

WRITING THE IMPLEMENTATION AND ANALYSIS SECTION

OBJECTIVES FOR THIS CHAPTER

- To explore the purpose of the implementation section
- To consider how to structure the implementation section
- To explore the features of a 'good' implementation section.

THE PURPOSE OF THE IMPLEMENTATION SECTION

In this chapter, we will consider the purpose of the implementation/analysis section and how it relates to the other sections of your written account. It is likely that this will be the most substantial section of your account, in terms of allocation of words, so it is important to understand what it should include. We will consider how you might structure this section, both as a whole and within subsections. Examples will be used to help you to identify what makes a 'good' implementation section, as well as exploring some common difficulties and how to avoid them.

If you have read some action research reports and engaged with other texts about undertaking action research, you may have noticed some variation in terminology when referring to different sections of the written account, particularly in relation to the implementation section; you may have seen it referred to as 'discussion', 'findings', 'evidence and analysis' or a number of other potential titles. Whatever its name, the section that we refer to as 'implementation' is crucial; indeed, Bell and Waters (2018: 322) identify it as 'the heart of the report'. Following on from the enquiry design section, in which you outlined how you intended to conduct the enquiry, the implementation section tells the story of the enquiry itself. In simple terms, you will discuss what you did, what happened and what you found out, but the reality is much more complex than this, as we will go on to discuss in more depth later in this chapter. A common pitfall is to only view this section in simple terms, which can result in an account that is overly descriptive and lacking in evidence to support claims made. While some level of description will be inevitable, this should be kept to a minimum, devoting the majority of the implementation section to analysis and evaluation, which should be evidence-based throughout.

STRUCTURE OF THE IMPLEMENTATION SECTION

As with all sections of your written account, it is helpful to briefly introduce your implementation section, outlining its purpose and how you intend to structure it. When considering how to structure this section, it is important to remember that you have undertaken action research, as opposed to any other kind of research; this distinction is important, as an appropriate structure when dealing with action research is rather different from the structure you might employ when dealing with other types of methodology. For many research types, this section is likely to be organised by themes (Roberts-Holmes, 2018) or by considering each enquiry objective in turn (Walliman and Buckler, 2016). However, action research is a cyclical journey, one in which each cycle influences the planning and teaching of the next cycle, through systematic reflection and action planning at the end of each cycle. It is therefore much more appropriate to present the implementation section of an action research study chronologically, focusing on each cycle in turn, as this will enable the writer to communicate explicitly their understanding of the action research process to the reader. Each cycle may relate to an individual lesson or short sequence of lessons, as explained in Chapter 9.

In itself this can lead to challenges, as you might therefore expect that you will discuss all of the cycles engaged in during the enquiry and, depending on the number of cycles and the number of words allowed, that might be perfectly appropriate. However, as Sharp (2012) identifies, you may well have too much material and need to be selective about what to include and what to leave out.

It is better to focus on fewer cycles and engage in deep, rigorous analysis and evaluation than to include all cycles and handle them superficially. Selecting which cycles to leave out may be straightforward: if a lesson is not relevant to your focus, there is no value in including it. However, selecting which cycles to leave out can be challenging, as there may not be an immediately obvious solution. If that is the case, you will need to return to the data for each cycle and possibly be quite ruthless in deciding which cycles are potentially the 'richest', in terms of your focus and enquiry objectives, and which add little value compared to others. Some new and aspiring teachers prefer to write the implementation including all cycles, then delete the less valuable ones if they find they are over the word limit; you may prefer to take this approach, but do bear in mind that it

inevitably wastes some of your time, in writing material which you later remove, and also requires some work and skill in ensuring that what remains still 'fits together' in a logical and coherent manner. Another way to approach deciding which cycles to leave out, if you have too much evidence, is to consider your conclusions at this stage: What have you learnt about your focus and how to do it effectively? If you can generate a list, you can then include the cycles that will provide the most convincing evidence in relation to your conclusions and leave out those that provide less. Therefore, the cycles you discuss in your implementation may not be consecutive but should still be chronological.

You can also structure this section at a deeper level, by utilising subsections within each cycle, which could be indicated through subheadings or the use of clear paragraphing. You should aim to include the following subsections for each cycle:

- **Objectives**: Outline the learning objectives for the lesson(s), remembering that these are not the same as enquiry objectives.
- **Content and approach**: Provide the reader with some information about the content of the session, keeping description to a necessary minimum (consider including plans within your appendices), including the approach taken in relation to your focus.
- **Analysis and evaluation of evidence**: Undertake some in-depth analysis of the evidence, focusing particularly on the impact on learning, and use this to inform evidence-based evaluation of your practice.
- **Summary**: Summarise your evaluation of your own practice and identify action points for the next cycle.

Each of these subsections will be explored in more detail in the next section of this chapter.

CRITICAL TASK 13.1

Remember Geoff from Chapter 2, the early years practitioner who wanted to improve his practice in engaging children in sustained shared thinking? He has started to write the implementation section of his written account of the enquiry. He is planning to include six cycles, as he has data for all of these. After writing about one cycle, Geoff realises that he has already used more than half of the suggested word limit for this section. What would you advise him to do at this point?

WRITING A 'GOOD' IMPLEMENTATION SECTION

As outlined above, it is most appropriate to structure the implementation section chronologically, focusing on each of the cycles you intend to include, in order. If you are missing some cycles out, it is helpful to explain this at the outset of the implementation section, stating clearly how you decided which to include and which to leave out.

INTRODUCING THE LEARNING OBJECTIVES

This is very useful information for the reader, in terms of understanding some of the planning and teaching decisions that you have taken. Given that you have already taught these lessons, the learning objectives should be easily retrieved from your plans.

CONTENT OF THE LESSON

There is great skill involved in providing the reader with sufficient information to 'set the scene', without providing too much description. If the reader does not have some understanding about the content of the lesson, they are unlikely to be able to follow your analysis of the evidence generated by the lesson. As long as you refer to it, you can include your planning documentation within your appendix, which will provide more information for the reader, if required. In particular, the reader needs to know the approach taken to your enquiry focus in this lesson.

CASE STUDY 13.1

Julie, a BEd primary student teacher, focused on improving her use of questioning to develop Year 1 children's mathematical reasoning; she wrote the following:

Aims:

- Employ a five second wait time.
- Extend reasoning skills using higher-order questions, such as 'how' or 'why'.

This was the second lesson focusing upon capacity, using estimation and testing with various sized bottles (Appendix C, highlighted in green). Once again, the activity was highly practical, particularly essential when teaching measurement (Cockcroft, 1982) and as Askew (2012) confirms, resources support children's reasoning, helping them to think through their answers to questions.

This short paragraph provides the reader with the necessary information about the content of the lesson and the approach taken related to her questioning in this particular lesson. To further improve this, Julie could have explicitly stated the learning objectives for the lesson, but these were easily accessible by referring to Appendix C.

PRESENTING AND ANALYSING THE EVIDENCE

Firstly, note that this does not mean providing and commenting upon evidence relating to every single aspect of the lesson. You must remain focused on the aspect of practice that you selected, so you therefore need to select critical incidents that are most relevant to your focus. If your focus is your use of questioning, then it is highly likely that you will need to present some evidence of the questions asked and how the children responded to these, probably in the form of 'transcriptlets'. The most significant aspect should be presented within the main body of the text, with a fuller version of the transcript provided within the appendix (again, remember that you must refer to it, if including it). However, you need to go beyond simply presenting the critical incidents and associated data: you need to 'unpick' the evidence. You need to explore what the children's responses tell you about their knowledge, understanding and skills. You should seek to link this to your own practice, relating to your focus. It is, however, important to be tentative in any claims that you make; children's responses, oral or written, do not always tell us the whole story about what they know, understand and can do. If a child has not included a particular piece of information in their response, that does not necessarily mean that the child does not know or understand it; the child may have omitted it for another reason. You also need to explore the other evidence and consider what this tells you about the children's learning. As discussed in Chapters 5 and 7, it can sometimes be helpful to make use of a focus group, rather than trying to discuss all children in the class. Avoid using phrases such as 'the children learnt to . . .' or 'the children all understood that . . .'; generalisations are rarely helpful and are difficult to support with evidence. Instead, comment on specific children: for example, 'Child A's response demonstrates that he understands . . . , as he has . . .'. This can feel uncomfortable, as you are probably acutely aware that you are responsible for the attainment and progress of all of the children in your class. That is why, though, in Chapters 5 and 7 we explained that all children should be treated equally and that the focus group should not be advantaged in any way. The purpose of having a focus group is to make the data collection and analysis more manageable. It is far more effective to analyse the learning of selected children in depth, rather than undertaking superficial analysis of the learning of all of the children in the class.

Even with a focus group, or by identifying and considering individual pupils at the point of writing, presenting evidence of learning can still require a significant proportion of your word limit. You can make use of your appendices to present evidence, but you need to avoid just pointing the reader in the direction of these. Be clear about which aspects of the included evidence are relevant to the point you are making within the discussion; you can annotate and/or highlight specific aspects to draw the reader's attention to them. You also need to ensure that your analysis is explicit, rather than implied (or left for the reader to do).

CASE STUDY 13.2

Compare these two excerpts from student work. In the second example, the student has analysed learning of specific children with explicit reference to detailed evidence, which is much stronger than the first example.

The children's work shows that they had made progress in their historical knowledge in this lesson (Appendix 12, 13, 14).

Joe's work shows that he had remembered some of the new facts introduced at the beginning of the lesson (Appendix 12, green highlighting), such as remembering that the fire started in a bakery: he wrote 'the fiyr it did sart in a Baicree' (sic). Lydia's work also includes some of the new facts (Appendix 13, green highlighting). Neither Joe nor Lydia include the date that the fire started, suggesting that they had not retained this information or that they neglected to include it; I noted, in my evaluation, that I needed to check this in the next lesson. Adam's work includes all of the new facts and he has also included the name of the baker, suggesting he has some prior knowledge, as this has not been addressed within the series of lessons (Appendix 14, green highlighting).

It is not for the reader to look at the appendices referred to and try to find and analyse the evidence that progress has been made in historical knowledge; you need to demonstrate this explicitly. The first excerpt in Case Study 13.2 includes the generic phrase 'the children', which needs to be avoided; you need to be precise about which children. As you can see, analysing the evidence in depth is time-consuming and uses far more words than taking a generic, evidence-free approach, so you need to be selective. If you are still struggling to incorporate all that you need to within the word limit, it may be possible to make use of organisational devices, such as tables, to present your evidence more concisely (graphs and other types of charts are unlikely to be of use in writing up this type of enquiry, as your data will be qualitative rather than quantitative). For example, you may include a table that indicates which success criteria each of the focus children met, or you may include a table that indicates which high-frequency, irregular words each of the focus children spelt correctly or incorrectly.

EVALUATING YOUR PRACTICE

You need to explore what all of the evidence tells you about your practice. Evaluate your effectiveness *in relation to your focus*. Try to avoid getting sidetracked into discussing other issues at length; for example, issues with managing behaviour will almost certainly impact on your effective use of lesson time and, if that is the case, should be explored as one of the factors, but you need to ensure your written account does not focus more heavily on managing behaviour than on using lesson time effectively. You need to include your analysis of the children's learning as part of the evidence to inform evaluation of your practice, but there will also be other evidence to consider, such as feedback from others. Remember that triangulating your evidence within the analysis will increase the validity of your study; referring to multiple sources of evidence when making claims will be more convincing to the reader and support a more nuanced analysis. As identified in Chapter 9, you will already have engaged in two layers of evaluation: immediately after the lesson and when reflecting on all of the evidence prior to planning the next cycle. As you write the implementation section of your enquiry, you will engage in a third layer of evaluation, as you may, with the benefit of hindsight, recognise issues or important factors that you did not previously identify; after all, you have probably now undertaken additional reading, as well as having the benefit of 'seeing the big picture', once the enquiry stage is complete. Coghlan (2019: 172) describes the writing phase as a 'whole new learning experience'. If you do recognise additional issues or important factors at this point, then it is perfectly appropriate to write about it in your implementation, but ensure that it is clear that you did not identify this at the time and that it therefore did not impact on your planning and teaching of the next cycle.

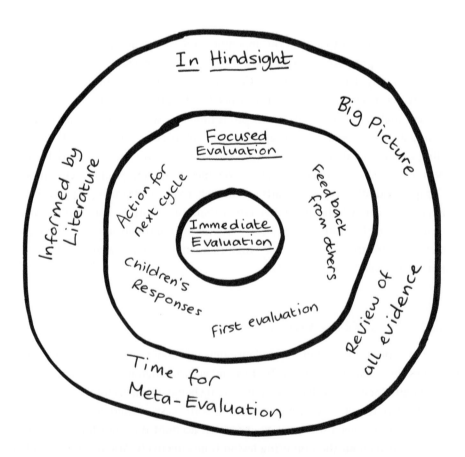

When evaluating your practice, you must support all of your claims with reference to evidence. Unsubstantiated claims are weak. You should also avoid being too self-congratulatory.

Be honest and be critical. A new teacher who is focusing on the effectiveness of their differentiation might use evidence that suggests all children met the learning objectives, in order to claim that their differentiation was therefore very effective. That might be the case, but it might also suggest that the learning objectives were not sufficiently challenging for all or some of the children. This possibility should also be explored, rather than simply concluding that your practice was exemplary. You should also return to your reading and the factors that you identified as potentially impacting on the selected focus.

CASE STUDY 13.3

Having noted that the open question that she asked at the start of the lesson prompted a number of valuable responses, Julie has considered less positive aspects of her questioning and has referred back to literature to support her discussion below:

> Moreover, it is apparent that the wait time rapidly decreased during the middle of the lesson when I posed seven questions consecutively (L27–L35). For example, after asking 'what is a millilitre?' (L29) I proceeded to ask, 'how much is a millilitre?' (L30) and 'how many millilitres are in this jug?' (L32). Both the closed nature of these questions and the non-existent wait time obtained no responses from the children. Aizikovitsh-Udi and Star (2011) inform that this approach hinders higher order thinking, indicating that in order to achieve my overarching aim I will need to increase the wait time and use more open, higher order questions such as 'how do you know that?' or 'why?', that facilitate more insightful responses (Haylock, 2010: 47–50).

> After further analysis of the transcript, it would appear that I predominantly asked closed questions (Appendix E2) and, in comparison to the open questions posed, these elicited limited responses. For example, when I asked, 'what are we going to use to help us find out?' (L33), only Imogen responded with a one-word answer of 'numbers' (L34).

Julie could have stopped at the point of identifying that her use of an open question was effective, but, as a critical learner, she was keen to explore further critical incidents (drawing in examples very effectively) in order to develop her practice further.

IDENTIFYING ADAPTATIONS TO YOUR PRACTICE FOR THE NEXT CYCLE

Within the enquiry design section of your written account, you will have demonstrated your understanding of the nature of action research, hopefully making reference to cycles where planning, teaching and reflection inform planning and teaching of the next cycle.

In the implementation section, you can demonstrate that this goes beyond a theoretical understanding, by making this absolutely explicit to the reader. One way of doing so is to conclude each cycle by outlining the action points that you identified for the next cycle.

CASE STUDY 13.4

Julie has demonstrated her understanding of the nature of action research by writing a concluding paragraph to outline the actions that she intends to take next:

After further analysis, it was evident that I improved the amount of wait time given (Appendix I). The children were given the opportunity to expand upon their ideas and to clarify their thinking before answering, which facilitated Chris and Wilf's ability to reason.

Although I developed my use of higher-order questions, this needs further practice. Questions will need to be progressive as it seems I was asking these too early, leading to confusion. Therefore, posing lower-order questions before those of a higher order may help to extend thinking (Wragg and Brown, 2001). Using a structure such as Bloom's Taxonomy (1952, cited in Sullivan, 2003) may assist me in developing this, coinciding with my rationale and the school's focus upon continuous professional development.

4.3 – Cycle three

Aims:

- Use a progressive structure of questioning, starting with lower order questions then building up to higher order questions.

By explicitly stating her aims at the start of the next cycle, it is very clear that Julie's evaluation has informed her planning for the next cycle.

WRITING UP SUBSEQUENT CYCLES

Subsequent cycles can be written up in exactly the same format as the first cycle. When you write up the final cycle, rather than identifying adaptations to your practice for the next cycle, you may identify potential adaptations for your future practice.

REFERRING TO LITERATURE

One of the factors that can distinguish a good implementation section from a less good one is the way in which literature is used. For some new and aspiring teachers, the idea of including literature within the implementation section can seem a little strange, given that you have already written a literature review. In fact, you are likely to be referring to the same literature sources again in the implementation section. As mentioned above, literature should be used to inform your evaluation, as Julie did so effectively when identifying the impact of her closed questions and lack of wait-time (see Case study 13.3). Remember that, in the literature review, you engaged with literature to develop and demonstrate your knowledge and understanding of the key factors involved in effective practice related to your selected focus. In the implementation section, you need to embed reference to literature throughout your discussion to demonstrate your understanding of the connections between what you read and your own practice. It is likely that your own experiences have mirrored much of what you read, but there may also be some differences and it is important to be critical when handling these; consider why your own experiences in your own practice did not match the literature.

RESPONSE TO CRITICAL TASK 13.1

If Geoff continues to write a similar amount for all six cycles, his work will be considerably over the word limit and no amount of careful editing will resolve such a significant issue. He needs to carefully consider whether he needs to include all six cycles, or whether there are some that can be left out. He should examine whether his writing is concise. He needs to explore whether he has included too much description, particularly in relation to the content of the lesson. Hopefully as you continued to read through this chapter, you realised that there are other things Geoff could do, such as consider the use of tables to present information succinctly and ensure that his evaluation is tightly focused and that he tracks specific children throughout, rather than trying to discuss all children.

SUMMARY FOR THIS CHAPTER

In this chapter, we have explored the purpose of the implementation section. It is important to remember that this goes beyond simply 'describing what happened'; it should involve evidence-based analysis and evaluation throughout. We have considered how to structure this section and what to include in order to ensure that you write a 'good' implementation section. After a brief introduction, you should discuss each of the cycles to be included in turn, identifying the learning objectives, the content of the lesson and the approach taken to your enquiry focus. You should then explore critical incidents from the lesson(s), undertaking detailed analysis of the evidence and evaluating your practice, drawing upon the evidence and literature to inform this. Each cycle should conclude with a summary of the effectiveness of your practice and how you intend to develop it in the next cycle. We have identified the importance of referring to literature, to ensure that the 'threads' identified in the literature review continue to run through the rest of the written account and to inform your evaluation. In the next chapter, we will consider how to write the conclusion to your action research report.

Do:

- organise this section chronologically, in cycles
- be selective about what to include, so that you can analyse and evaluate in depth
- draw upon evidence frequently, importing critical aspects within the discussion itself and supporting this with reference to appendices
- 'unpick' the evidence, making your analysis and evaluation explicit
- highlight and/or annotate the relevant aspects of appended evidence
- refer back to the literature to support your discussion
- remain focused (enquiry focus, focus group).

Don't:

- include too much lengthy description
- try to cover too much (too many cycles, too many children)
- expect the reader to analyse the evidence for you
- write in generic terms.

FURTHER READING

The following texts may also support you in writing your implementation section:

Cottrell, S. (2019) *The Study Skills Handbook.* 5th edn. Basingstoke: Palgrave Macmillan.

This text includes a useful table in Chapter 12 which summarises the differences between descriptive writing and critical, analytical writing.

Holliday, A. (2016) *Doing and Writing Qualitative Research.* 3rd edn. London: Sage.

Chapter 8 of this text offers some useful insights into making use of evidence to support claims and ensuring that claims are appropriate.

Richards, L. (2015) *Handling Qualitative Data: A Practical Guide.* 3rd edn. London: Sage.

Chapter 10 of this text provides useful guidance about writing the account of your action research enquiry. Emphasis is placed on the way in which evidence may be integrated into the implementation and analysis section.

14

WRITING THE CONCLUSION TO YOUR ACTION RESEARCH REPORT

OBJECTIVES FOR THIS CHAPTER

- To explore the purpose and content of the final chapter of the action research report
- To consider how to summarise the key findings of your action research study
- To explore how to reflect on the strengths and limitations of your study.

THE PURPOSE OF THE FINAL CHAPTER OF THE ACTION RESEARCH REPORT

In this chapter, we will consider how to finish your action research report with a strong final chapter or section. This is about doing more than just providing a summary of findings, as an effective conclusion should seek to continue to demonstrate academic criticality in relation to evidence, literature and the research process itself.

The final chapter of the action research report should also provide an opportunity to present a summary of your learning as a result of your enquiry and to reflect on the implications of the findings in relation to both future research and your developing practice. In many ways, the writing of this final chapter or section should be a pleasure, as it is an opportunity to reflect on how much your teaching has developed as a result of the enquiry and to look to the future and the impact your work will have on your practice in the early stages of your teaching career.

A POSSIBLE STRUCTURE FOR THE SUMMARY OR REVIEW OF FINDINGS

One neat way of reviewing your findings is to return to the objectives stated at the outset of the project and summarise what your evidence has revealed about each of these in turn. This provides an element of symmetry to the written account, with the objectives from the first chapter returned to in the final chapter, and enables you to be explicit about the alignment of the report from the beginning to the end.

This structure also provides another explicit opportunity to engage critically with the literature, as you can compare your own findings with those from published works and research reports. There is no need here to introduce new literature; you should return to the academic works that you reviewed earlier in the piece and identify where your evidence is aligned to or diverges from the established views.

In creating your summary of findings, it is important that the claims you make are clearly based on the evidence that you have already explored in the preceding section or chapter. It is useful here to refer back to specific examples from your analysis that the reader is already familiar with and which illustrate the key claims you wish to make related to your objectives. It is not necessary (and not advised) to draw new evidence into your account at this stage. The summary of findings really should draw together elements of the work that have already gone before, in relation to the objectives from the first section or chapter of the piece, the literature from the second section or chapter and the evidence presented in the fourth section or chapter.

CASE STUDY 14.1

In this example, Julie, a BEd primary student teacher, has been examining the impact of her questions on the development of primary children's mathematical reasoning. She has reviewed her first objective, and in this extract she is reviewing the second and third objectives together, rather than separately, as they are so closely interrelated. In doing so, she returns to a significant source from her literature review and compares her own findings to those from the published source. She reminds the reader of an example from her own evidence, which she has already explored in the previous chapter of her work, that illustrates and supports her claim. She is careful to avoid being self-congratulatory in summarising her findings, reminding the reader that simply following a certain approach will not always yield the hoped-for response, which leads to further enquiry as to why this might be. Note that, throughout this section, she is suitably tentative about her findings, as she recognises that she has limited evidence and that there are many ways to interpret qualitative evidence.

Findings in relation to objectives two and three:

- to analyse children's responses to my questions
- to evaluate my questioning and its impact on children's mathematical reasoning.

Chapter 4 demonstrates a critical analysis of my questioning and its impact upon children's reasoning skills. Cotton (2010) suggests that 'how' or 'why' questions are most effective in developing children's reasoning skills, as they require children to explain their thinking. Cycle two demonstrates that when these questions were posed, children elaborated, evidenced through Jim's extended answers and ability to reason using the word 'because' to justify his answers (pp. 39/40). These responses may reveal that using higher order questions promotes mathematical reasoning. Although these higher order questions seemed to elicit insightful, extended responses at times, other children's responses, such as Jenny's response of 'ummm' (p. 40), may indicate that these could have been posed too early.

CRITICAL TASK 14.1

In this example, Tim, a PGCE primary student teacher, is reviewing his enquiry in which he planned to develop his teaching skills in using resources to support differentiated learning in geography. Compare this example with that in Case study 14.1 and suggest ways in which Tim might improve this review of his findings.

This research has shown me how the quality of resources and the planning around the use of resources can impact teaching for better or worse. I have learned to make sure that all resources are differentiated to suit each learner's needs. This was demonstrated in lesson three where some of the children were unable to access and comprehend the role-play cards, making the subsequent activities difficult.

A POSSIBLE STRUCTURE FOR THE REST OF THE CONCLUSION

The final sections of the report should focus on the quality of the action research you have undertaken and the implications of your enquiry for future research and your practice as a teacher.

REVIEW OF RESEARCH METHODS

Remember that an important ethical principle of action research is that your enquiry should be undertaken as openly and honestly as possible and this applies just as much to the review of your study as to the earlier stages of the project. In this section of your report, you should aim to reflect on the strengths and, perhaps more importantly, as advised by McNiff (2016a), on the limitations of your study, with reference to appropriate education research literature, and make suggestions on how your enquiry might have been more robust as a piece of research. This would normally relate to the quality and relevance of the evidence, but may also relate to subtle ethical issues which, with the benefit of hindsight, you feel could have been managed more effectively, or to the approach you chose to take to analyse your data. In this section, you should aim to maintain the critical approach adopted throughout the written report and make practical and realistic suggestions as to how your study could have been more effective as a piece of action research; as Hyatt (2004: 53) notes, 'admitting them [limitations] does not suggest a weakness in your work, rather it illustrates that you are thinking about your work critically'.

VALIDITY

It is common to reflect on the validity of the enquiry, with consideration of the range of data gathered, and to suggest ways in which this could have been more robust or provided more detailed or relevant evidence. For example, depending on the focus of the enquiry, it may be that you can identify that it would have been beneficial to make use of audio-recording of conversations rather than rely on the making of observational notes, and why this would have been of more benefit.

ANALYSIS

It is less common, but just as valuable, to evaluate the ways in which you engaged in analysis of your evidence, which may relate to the way in which you selected appropriate evidence from the data or the way in which you chose to interrogate the evidence. For example, you may reflect on the level of detail to which you analysed samples of pupils' written work or the way in which you extracted meaning from transcripts of your teaching and pupils' responses.

ETHICS

Similarly, it is important to reflect on your management of both obvious and subtle ethical issues throughout the project and the ways in which you ensured the project itself did not impact negatively on any learners or, indeed, unfairly advantage one group or individual over others, and on the steps that you took to be open and transparent about your enquiry. You might, for example, reflect on the extent to which you shared the project with the children or young people involved; at the outset of an action research project, it is easy to either overlook or downplay the importance of explaining your research to the learners and, on reflection, you may feel that you could and should have done more to be clear about your purpose and the focus of your enquiry.

As explored in Chapters 5 and 7, a valuable way of being open about your enquiry and bringing a kind of closure to your project is to share your key findings with some colleagues in your school or setting. This might be in the form of a presentation but could just as valuably be in the form of a conversation with one or two members of the team

that you have worked with. New teachers can sometimes feel that their action research has not revealed anything 'new' or even 'interesting' and may be reluctant, therefore, to share their findings, but a conversation about what they have learnt about themselves and about the endless joys and challenges of teaching and learning will be interesting to the vast majority of teachers. On this point, while the reliability of your study will be low (due to the small sample size), there is likely to be a degree of 'recognisability' in your findings, in which teaching colleagues might understand or recognise aspects for discussion.

This kind of openness is important in terms of being respectful to the colleagues who have supported you and enabled your project to take place, but may also provide a good opportunity to discuss the evidence that underpins your findings and to review its validity. In effect, this discussion should help to both clarify your findings and support you in reflecting on the effectiveness of your study as a piece of action research. As such, it is a final opportunity to gather some triangulated evidence, in the form of your colleagues' responses and feedback, to add validity to your findings, and this might be reported on, briefly, in this final section.

CRITICAL TASK 14.2

In this example, Tim is reviewing the limitations of his study, which focused on his use of resources to support differentiation. What do you think of his critique?

The evidence in this study focused on children of a range of attainment levels. I believe that my examples of children's work and the analysis of work focused on the higher attaining children more than on the other children. I found that, when analysing the work, I had more to consider and make claims about from the evidence for the higher attaining children when compared to the others. Analysing the effectiveness of resources should take into account all children's learning equally and this is an area of the study that could have been improved.

CASE STUDY 14.2

In this example, Julie is reviewing the quality of her study as a piece of research. Note that, while she is largely content with her chosen methods, she is still aiming to be critical through suggesting some specific ways in which the enquiry could have been more rigorous and noting the limitations of the size of the study.

The data collection methods were suitable and the audio transcripts provided significant insight into the children's developing reasoning skills. However, these did not record non-verbal aspects such as body language, which may have given more depth to my analysis (Cohen et al., 2011). Additionally, I recognize that, at times, I was unable to triangulate my findings through additional observations and examples of children's work (Koshy, 2010). Therefore, in order to make my findings more reliable in future, I need to collect a greater range of evidence. The limitations of this study and the small scale in which it was conducted make it challenging to generalise my findings.

FUTURE RESEARCH

It is important to be realistic about any recommendations you make about future research. The intention here is to make suggestions not so much of research that others might do (such as 'there needs to be more research on the impact of feedback on children's self-esteem') but on where you might take your own learning next. This does not need to be through another formally assessed action research project but might be based on a similarly evidence-based, evaluative approach.

It could be that the next steps for research might relate to some of the literature that you engaged with as part of your action research enquiry. There may be some published research that piqued your interest during your reading or of which you feel you only just started to scratch the surface in relation to your own practice or understanding. For example, you may have been focusing on developing the children's or young people's higher-order thinking and identified some recent research on this which you would like to explore further.

IMPACT ON PRACTICE DURING THE STUDY AND IN FUTURE TEACHING

Finally, a great way to conclude your written report is to reflect on your own professional learning and, in particular, to identify the impact that the enquiry has had on your own development as a new teacher. This does not need to be a long section, but it is important, nonetheless, to provide some symmetry for your account by returning to the rationale for undertaking your enquiry and reflecting on what you have learnt, the extent to which your teaching has improved as a result and the implications for your future teaching.

RESPONSE TO CRITICAL TASK 14.1

We suggested that you compare this example with that in Case study 14.1 and suggest ways in which Tim might improve this review of his findings.

> This research has shown me how the quality of resources and the planning around the use of resources can impact teaching for better or worse. I have learned to make sure that all resources are differentiated to suit each learner's needs. This was demonstrated in lesson three where some of the children were unable to access and comprehend the role-play cards, making the subsequent activities difficult.

In reviewing his enquiry objectives and summarising his findings, Tim should aim to be as specific as possible about what was revealed through the analysis of his evidence and to avoid making statements that any teacher could make without undertaking a piece of action research – most of us could say that the quality of resources and how they are used are likely to have an impact on the quality of learning or that resources should be matched to the abilities of the learners. It would have been more focused for Tim to state some specific findings, with specific examples drawn in from the previous section, about how best to use resources to meet individual needs and how to engage learners in using resources independently to support their own learning. Tim should also aim to return to relevant, significant literature from his literature review section, in order to make comparisons with his own findings.

RESPONSE TO CRITICAL TASK 14.2

In this example, Tim is reviewing the limitations of his study, which focused on his use of resources to support differentiation. We asked you what you think of his critique.

> The evidence in this study focused on children of a range of attainment levels. I believe that my examples of children's work and the analysis of work focused on the higher attaining children more than on the other children. I found that, when analysing the work, I had more to consider and make claims about from the evidence for the higher attaining children when compared to the others. Analysing the effectiveness of resources should take into account all children's learning equally and this is an area of the study that could have been improved.

Tim has identified an important issue, in critiquing his action research enquiry, which relates to the quality of his study: there is an ethical aspect to it, and this clearly relates to his future practice in planning to meet a range of needs within his class. On reflection, he has identified some bias in his analysis of data; he probably was not aware of this as he undertook his study, given the busy demands of his school placement, but it is a valuable point to identify about how the enquiry could have been enhanced. In any study, the author makes countless decisions about which elements from the body of their data will be selected as evidence and drawn into their account to form the basis for their analysis; being aware of any potential bias throughout the process is important, but it is also worth reviewing the project at its conclusion, as Tim has, to consider whether any possible bias has inadvertently crept into the process. Some new and aspiring teachers worry about pointing out the limitations in their own work, particularly if it is an assessed piece of work, but identifying and being honest about them, just as Tim has done, is seen as a positive aspect of the work; it is far better than the reader or marker spotting the limitations for you.

SUMMARY FOR THIS CHAPTER

In this chapter, we have considered how to write an effective final chapter or section to your action research report, through reviewing or summarising your findings, in relation to your stated objectives, and comparing these to the established literature. We have noted the importance of reviewing the quality of your own research, with reference to literature on educational research, and how you might have improved the rigour or validity of your study. Finally, we have considered the importance, in this section of the work, of reflecting on your own professional learning as a new teacher and of considering the implications of your enquiry for future practice.

In the concluding chapter of the book, we will explore some features of effective academic writing and consider some possible next steps for new teachers who have recently completed an action research enquiry and wish to take this further.

Do:

- return to your objectives to provide a framework for reviewing your findings
- relate your findings to those in the published literature
- review the strengths and limitations of your study as a piece of research
- consider how your research could be developed in the future
- summarise the impact of the study on your development as a new teacher.

Don't:

- introduce any new evidence
- introduce any new literature
- make claims that are not clearly based on the preceding discussion
- set unrealistic goals for future research.

FURTHER READING

McNiff, J. (2016) *Writing Up Your Action Research Project*. Abingdon: Routledge.

Part 3 of this book provides helpful guidance on how the quality of an action research report might be judged and how this might influence the way the report is written.

Punch, K. and Oancea, A. (2014) *Introduction to Research Methods in Education*. 2nd edn. London: Sage.

This comprehensive book is useful for reference at almost any stage of the research process and includes a helpful section on how to evaluate an enquiry.

Wilson, E. (2017) 'Writing about research', in E. Wilson (ed.), *School-based Research: A Guide for Education Students*. 3rd edn. London: Sage, pp. 295–311.

This helpful chapter provides guidance on the process of communicating your research process through a written report.

15

CONCLUSION

OBJECTIVES FOR THIS CHAPTER

- To reflect on the longer-term benefits of undertaking an action research enquiry
- To provide some guidance about effective and clear academic writing
- To offer some thoughts about possible next steps, including masters, doctorates and publications.

SOME REFLECTIONS ON ACTION RESEARCH

In this, the final chapter, we will reflect on the issues explored throughout the book and consider how the experience of undertaking an action research enquiry might impact on your future development, both professionally and academically. We will also explore some issues related to writing effectively, which should be helpful in the writing of an action research report and throughout your career as a professional educator.

We have, throughout the book, established the benefits for the new teacher in undertaking an action research project. As noted by Sagor (2011), it enables you to examine the detail of an aspect of your practice in an evidence-based and rigorous manner so that you can bring about meaningful improvements to your teaching and the learning of the children or young people that you teach.

However, action research also provides a model or way of approaching evaluation beyond the timeframe of a specific project. The principles of reflecting on practice on the basis of evidence and of using the children's learning as the main test of the effectiveness of your teaching will be valuable throughout your career. We agree with McNiff (2017: 198): 'For me, action research is not only about doing projects, it is more about living a life of enquiry'. It is not necessary to undertake a 'full' action research project, complete with objectives, research plan and literature review, in order to identify an aspect of your practice to develop and look critically at the impact of your approach on outcomes for learners. Embedding an evidence-based approach into your evaluation of teaching and learning will not only enhance the quality of your teaching but also prepare you for taking on more responsibility as your career develops. As a subject or curriculum coordinator, or a leader of whole-school initiatives, the same principles of action research will underpin a robust approach to school improvement through understanding the impact of current practice on learning and carefully evaluating the impact of developments on outcomes for learners.

SOME GUIDANCE ON ACADEMIC WRITING

If you have engaged thoroughly in a rigorous action research process and are clear about how you will present this to create an effective written report, you will want to ensure that your work is as free of errors as possible. Having marked literally thousands of assignments, we are well placed to advise on the characteristics of good academic writing and on some of the common errors in students' written work, as well as how you can avoid them. We will consider this in relation to issues of substance, related to the quality of academic writing, and issues of style, related to presentation and clarity.

ISSUES OF SUBSTANCE

There are other books available on the theme of academic writing, so here we just identify some of the key nuggets of advice that we offer our students to help them develop confidence and effectiveness in the quality of their academic writing.

ATTEND TO ASSESSMENT CRITERIA

The best advice that we can give students about their academic writing is they should aim to *make every sentence earn its place* in their report. This means attending very carefully to the stated criteria by which your work will be judged and ensuring that every sentence is contributing something in relation to them. Criteria for writing at Level Six (final year of undergraduate degrees) and Level Seven (postgraduate/master's level) rarely include words such as 'descriptive', 'repetitive' or 'rambling' and more commonly include words such as 'analytical', 'evaluative' and 'critical', so you should aim to keep the descriptive elements of your work to the necessary minimum and maximise those elements that will earn credit in the marking process. Some description may be necessary when outlining the content and teaching approach taken within a particular learning episode, but you should aim to keep this as brief as possible to enable you to move on quickly to analysis of learning and evaluation of practice.

COMMUNICATE CLEARLY

You want your reader to understand your message in just one reading, so the more you can do to guide them about the structure of the work and your reasons for presenting it as you have, the easier it will be for them to access it and follow your thinking.

You should start every section or chapter of your written report with an introductory paragraph setting out both the purpose and structure. This is not just a nicety for the benefit of the marker or for padding out the text to help you reach the required word count. It is also beneficial for you, the writer, to be absolutely clear about what you are trying to achieve at every point of the report and how, through your writing, you are doing so. Similarly, it is valuable to write a brief conclusion for each section or chapter before moving on to the next, so that you can be clear about what you have achieved and the main points that you have established so far.

Focus on just one issue in each paragraph. Academic writing becomes difficult for the reader to follow when several issues are dealt with all at once in the same section. Giving your writing a coherent structure will be beneficial for you in the writing and for the reader in the reading.

BE ACADEMICALLY RIGOROUS

You should aim to avoid making unsubstantiated claims. Whenever you make any claim, it is a good idea to ask yourself how you would defend the claim if someone were to challenge it or, in other words, how you know that your claim is 'true'. This is as true in the literature review as it is when presenting your own findings, as claims in this section should be clearly and explicitly based on the sources you have reviewed.

Similarly, try to avoid saying 'I feel' or 'I felt', at any point, as your report should be as objective as possible and you should therefore base your analysis and claims on evidence rather than on your feelings. Intuition probably is important in teaching, but in action research, evidence is the key.

Aim to avoid what Bassey (1995: 77) describes as sandbagging: 'adding to a statement inert defences to make it look secure'. This is where the writer makes a statement and then puts an author's name in brackets at the end, without making it entirely clear what they are attributing to that author.

It almost (but, sadly, not quite) goes without saying that you should aim to avoid plagiarism (that is, using the intellectual property of others without appropriate acknowledgement) and other forms of poor academic practice, such as borrowing chunks from an acknowledged source without being clear that these are direct quotes. It is important to reference carefully and this should not be seen as a rather dry test of your technical academic skills, but as part of your ongoing quest to present a report to the highest ethical standards. The ethic of respect for truth requires us to be open and honest about where the work of others is incorporated into our own.

ISSUES OF STYLE

It is important to present your work as well as possible. As a teacher you are a professional communicator, and that should apply to your written communication as much as your verbal communication, so issues of style are important.

DEMARCATION

Most students are aware of the need to use paragraphs in their academic writing and these should be clearly demarcated through leaving a clear space between one and the next. This makes the writing easier to access and follow.

Sentences should also be clearly demarcated, using full stops and capital letters. However, there should be no full stop after titles or subheadings. This makes sense when you stop to think about it, as a title or subheading is not, normally, a complete sentence and does not need to be treated as such.

DEALING WITH NUMBERS

Since your report is a piece of formal, academic writing, you should write small and uncomplicated numbers as words rather than numerals. For example, you should write 'there were seven children in the group' rather than 'there were 7 children in the group'. Larger numbers may be written as figures, as it can get complicated to write 1,274 as one thousand, two hundred and seventy-four.

CRITICAL TASK 15.1

Here is a short extract from a student's assignment. What advice would you give them about the academic substance of their work?

> Having looked at the children's books, I felt that many were making good progress, although one or two were struggling (Forster, 2010). In common with most teachers, I believe that differentiation by outcome is the most effective approach, and so planned for this in the subsequent lesson.

SOME COMMON PROBLEMS WITH GRAMMAR AND PUNCTUATION

Here are some things to remember about punctuation and grammar and some of the errors that we have noted over the years, in no particular order.

APOSTROPHES

Apostrophes have two main functions: to show where one or more letters have been omitted and to indicate possession. Apostrophes showing omission are rare in academic writing, as it is normal to avoid contracted forms such as *can't* or *don't*, so the main problems with apostrophes normally relate to possession. Possession by a single person or object is usually indicated by an apostrophe followed by the letter *s*, as in the following examples:

John's work was beautifully presented.

This child's answer was intriguing.

Possession by more than one person or object (words that normally end in *s*) is usually indicated by an apostrophe after the *s* at the end of the word. However, some plural words

(Continued)

do not end in s (*children* being a particularly relevant example), and in these cases an apostrophe followed by the letter s is used. Note the position of the apostrophe in these two examples, both of which refer to more than one learner:

The pupils' understanding of long division was impressive.

The children's understanding of long division was impressive.

There are some exceptions to the use of the possessive apostrophe and the one that trips students up most frequently relates to the word 'it'. When showing possession of 'it', no possessive apostrophe is required, as in the following example:
The bag split and its contents spilled out.

FULL STOPS, COMMAS, COLONS AND SEMICOLONS

It is worth developing a confident and precise approach to the use of punctuation marks, as these enable the reader to follow your meaning more easily.
Full stops are usually well understood, but academic work can sometimes introduce some confusions that are not present in other forms of writing. For example, some students are not sure where to put the full stop when their sentence ends with brackets, so it is worth remembering that the full stop goes after the brackets, as in this example:

I decided to use pencil-free homework (Forster et al., 2010).

A similar issue arises when a sentence ends with an embedded quote. In academic writing, the full stop comes after the quote mark, as in the following example:

Forster and Eperjesi (2021: 182) suggest that 'a sentence should typically end with a full stop'.

Commas are used to indicate where the reader might take a brief pause in reading. However, this does not mean that they can be sprinkled wherever you wish within your writing. A particular use of the comma that can cause some difficulty relates to subordinate clauses. A subordinate clause is a phrase that is embedded within a sentence and which, if removed, leaves a sentence that is complete; it is sometimes read in a slightly lower tone of voice than the rest of the sentence. The subordinate clause should have a comma at each end. Sometimes, a subordinate clause comes at the beginning of a sentence and is indicated with just one comma. Here are some examples, with the subordinate clause indicated in italics. Notice the placement of the commas.

A subordinate clause, *such as this*, should have a comma at each end.

For various reasons, a subordinate clause can sometimes come at the beginning of a sentence.

Colons and semicolons have specific uses and should not be confused. The main function of the semicolon is to connect two complete sentences that are closely related and could normally be replaced with a full stop or a connective, as in the following example:

> The main function of the semicolon is to connect two complete sentences that are closely related; it could normally be replaced with a full stop or a connective.

The semicolon cannot be replaced by a comma, as this would result in a run-on sentence (also known as a comma-splice), another error that occurs frequently in assignments we mark.

The main function of the colon is to indicate that the second part of a sentence will in some way explain or exemplify the first part, as in the following example:

> A colon has one main function: to indicate that the second part of the sentence explains or exemplifies the first.

SOME COMMON SPELLING ERRORS

The use of a spellchecker will help to avoid many spelling errors, but there are still some words that might slip through, so it is worth being clear on these. Here are just three examples of these tricky words.

Lead and *led*: the past tense of lead is *led*, whereas *lead* is a soft metal.

Effect and *affect* (as verbs): to *affect* something means to have an influence on it, whereas to *effect* something means to achieve it or complete it.

Effect and *affect* (as nouns): an *effect* is the impact something has whereas *affect* relates to feelings or emotions.

Practice and *practise*: in most contexts, *practice* is a noun and *practise* is a verb.

It is worth noting that a spellchecker will miss some typographical errors, where the error is another real word. One common example is *from* and *form*. Using the 'find' tool to search for these words will enable you to check they have been used as intended.

CREATING A TITLE

It is surprising how stressful it can be to create an appropriate title for your assignment or dissertation. We would normally advise that you leave the exact wording flexible until very near the end of the writing process; so long as, from the beginning, you are very clear about what you are trying to achieve, the title will probably sort itself out towards the end. There are, broadly, two choices: you can opt for either a question or a statement. In either case, remember to keep in mind the overarching aim of improving your practice, which should be reflected in the title. Avoid phrasing your title in such a way that suggests you were trying to find out the 'best' way of doing something or comparing strategies or approaches.

Some examples:

> An investigation into my use of concrete apparatus to support lower attaining children in their understanding of fractions
>
> How can I facilitate peer talk in problem-solving to develop higher attaining pupils' mathematical reasoning?
>
> Improving questioning to develop higher order thinking in Year 10 geography students: an action research study

YOUR NEXT STEPS IN PERSONAL DEVELOPMENT AND ACTION RESEARCH

Action research is a bit like marmite: some people really enjoy the process of grappling with their evidence and identifying ways in which their practice had an impact on learning and considering ways in which they could improve their teaching, while, for others, an action research study undertaken as part of their initial teacher education programme is the last they hope to complete. This last section is really aimed at the former group.

If you have enjoyed the process of undertaking and writing up an action research project, then you might like to take this a stage further by undertaking a master's degree in education. The early stage of your career is a great time to engage in some explicit professional development, and action research is well embedded as a research approach in many master's programmes and, if you enjoy that, then you may even consider undertaking a doctorate.

If, through action research, you have discovered something significant in the teaching and learning process then you might like to share your findings through publishing an article in a journal, such as *Educational Action Research* or the *Student Teacher Perspective Journal*.

RESPONSE TO CRITICAL TASK 15.1

This student has asked you for some advice about the academic substance of their work.

> Having looked at the children's books, I felt that many were making good progress, although one or two were struggling (Forster, 2010). In common with most teachers, I believe that differentiation by outcome is the most effective approach, and so planned for this in the subsequent lesson.

In this short section, there are several issues worth addressing.

1. The first sentence would have been enhanced through making explicit reference to the evidence from the children's work and the criteria by which judgements about progress were made. Some examples from the evidence, drawn into the text, would help to make the case more clearly, particularly in relation to the specific aspects that the 'one or two' were struggling with, as these exceptions are important to inform the next learning episode. This would make the claim about progress more robust and not based purely on a 'feeling'.

2. There is some sandbagging, as it is not clear what is being attributed to Forster (2010). The student teacher should either remove the reference, as it serves no purpose in its current form, or be explicit about how the work of Forster was useful in analysing the children's learning or evaluating the teacher's practice.

3. Finally, there is an unsubstantiated claim. How does the student teacher know that most teachers think that differentiation by outcome is the most effective approach, and even if they do *believe* this, does this provide a robust, evidence-informed basis with which to inform his practice?

SUMMARY FOR THIS CHAPTER

In this chapter, we have reflected on the benefits of undertaking an action research project and on taking the action research approach with you throughout your career. We have explored how you might develop your interest and expertise in evidence-informed improvement of practice through undertaking a higher degree or disseminating your learning through publications. We have also considered some rather mundane but important issues related to writing well; again, these are useful in the writing of your action research report but will also be valuable throughout the rest of your career, as you seek to become a clear and highly effective communicator.

We hope that this book has been of some benefit to you in reflecting on your practice and we wish you well as you seek to become an outstanding teacher.

Do:

*   enjoy your action research enquiries and your teaching
*   take the evidence-based approach to improving teaching and learning throughout your career
*   aim to write clearly, concisely and precisely
*   consider your next steps.

Don't:

- leave it to the last minute to start writing
- forget to proof-read before submission
- allow minor errors to detract from the overall quality of your work.

FURTHER READING

The following sources may also support you in completing your report to a high standard and looking ahead to future development:

McGrath, J. and Coles, A. (2015) *Your Education Masters Companion: The Essential Guide to Success*. Abingdon: Routledge.

This recent publication is a comprehensive guide to undertaking a master's in education and includes a helpful list of the 'top ten mistakes to avoid'. For those considering embarking on a master's in education, the early chapters will be valuable for helping understand what is involved and why the time and effort invested in undertaking a higher degree should be worthwhile.

Medwell, J., Wray, D., Moore, G. and Griffiths, V. (2017) *Primary English: Knowledge and Understanding*. 8th edn. London: Sage/Learning Matters.

This key text for all primary teachers of English includes some very useful chapters to develop your knowledge and understanding of grammar and punctuation.

Sinclair, C. (2010) *Grammar: A Friendly Approach*. 2nd edn. Maidenhead: Open University Press, McGraw Hill Education.

This useful book addresses aspects of writing with precision and confidence, including, of course, guidance on grammar and punctuation.

The Student Teacher Perspective (STeP) Journal is published by the Teacher Education Advancement Network, based at the University of Cumbria, and provides an excellent opportunity to read the work of student teachers and to make your own contribution through sharing your own enquiry findings. It is available online and worth reviewing regularly.

REFERENCES

Bassey, M. (1995) *Creating Education Through Research: A Global Perspective of Educational Research for the 21st Century*. Newark: Kirklington Moor Press and Edinburgh: British Educational Research Association.

Bell, J. and Waters, S. (2018) *Doing Your Research Project: A Guide for First-time Researchers*. 7th edn. Maidenhead: Open University Press.

Black, P. and Wiliam, D. (1990) *Inside the Black Box: Raising Standards through Classroom Assessment*. London: King's College.

British Educational Research Association (BERA) (2018) *Ethical Guidelines for Educational Research*. 4th edn. London: BERA. Available at: www.bera.ac.uk/publications/ethical-guidelines (accessed 17 June 2020).

Brooks, R., te Riele, K. and Maguire, M. (2014) *Ethics and Education Research*. London: Sage.

Brown, D. (2019) 'Framing the research', in C. Opie and D. Brown (eds), *Getting Started in Your Educational Research: Design, Data Production and Analysis*. London: Sage. pp. 39–54.

Chartered College of Teaching (n.d.) *About Us*. Available at: https://chartered.college/aboutus/ (accessed 14 July 2020).

Coghlan, D. (2019) *Doing Action Research in Your Own Organisation*. 5th edn. London: Sage.

Cohen, L., Manion, L. and Morrison, K. (2018) *Research Methods in Education*. 8th edn. London: Sage.

Department for Education (DfE) (2012) *Teachers' Standards*. London: Her Majesty's Stationery Office.

Education Endowment Foundation (EEF) (2020) *Metacognition and Self-regulated Learning: Summary of Recommendations* poster. London: Education Endowment Foundation.

Eperjesi, R. (2020) 'Art and design: modelling to promote creativity', in C. Forster and R. Eperjesi (eds), *Teaching the Primary Curriculum*. London: Sage, pp. 11–27.

Evans, M. (2017) 'Reliability and validity in qualitative research by teacher researchers', in E. Wilson (ed.), *School-based Research: A Guide for Education Students*. 3rd edn. London: Sage, pp. 202–16.

Ewens, T. (2014) *Reflective Primary Teaching*. Northwich: Critical Publishing.

Fisher, J. (2016) *Interacting or Interfering? Improving Interactions in the Early Years.* Maidenhead: Open University Press.

Forster, C. and Penny, J. (2020) 'Science: questioning skilfully to promote intelligent answers', in C. Forster and R. Eperjesi (eds), *Teaching the Primary Curriculum.* London: Sage, pp. 224–37.

Foulger, A. (2010) 'External conversations: an unexpected discovery about the critical friend in action research enquiries', *Action Research*, 8 (2): 135–52.

Hattie, J. (2009) *Visible Learning: A Synthesis of Over 800 Meta-analyses Relating to Achievement.* Abingdon: Routledge.

Hattie, J. (2012) *Visible Learning for Teachers: Maximizing Impact on Learning.* Abingdon: Routledge.

Holliday, A. (2016) *Doing and Writing Qualitative Research.* 3rd edn. London: Sage.

Howells, K. and Gregory, P. (2016) 'Data analysis', in R. Austin (ed.), *Researching Primary Education.* London: Sage/Learning Matters, pp. 93–111.

Hyatt, D. (2004) 'Writing research', in C. Opie (ed.), *Doing Educational Research: A Guide to First-time Researchers.* London: Sage, pp. 34–57.

Kay, L. (2019) 'Guardians of research: negotiating the strata of gatekeepers in research with vulnerable participants', *PRACTICE*, 1 (1): 37–52.

Kay, L. (2020) 'Pivoting the seesaw? Negotiating the tensions of balancing ethical and methodological considerations in designing research that involves children and young people', *PRACTICE*, 2 (1): 21–32.

Koshy, V. (2010) *Action Research for Improving Educational Practice.* 2nd edn. London: Sage.

Lewis, J. and McNaughton Nicholls, C. (2014) 'Design issues', in J. Ritchie, L. Lewis, C. McNaughton Nicholls and R. Ormston (eds), *Qualitative Research Practice: A Guide for Social Science Students and Researchers.* London: Sage, pp. 47–76.

Lowe, S. and Harris, K. (2018) 'Short, medium and long-term planning', in H. Cooper and S. Elton-Chalcraft (eds), *Professional Studies in Primary Education.* 3rd edn. London: Sage, pp. 66–94.

McNiff, J. (2016a) *Writing Up Your Action Research Project.* Abingdon: Routledge.

McNiff, J. (2016b) *You and Your Action Research Project.* 4th edn. Abingdon: Routledge.

McNiff, J. (2017) *Action Research: All You Need to Know.* London: Sage.

McNiff, J. and Whitehead, J. (2005) *Action Research for Teachers: A Practical Guide.* Abingdon: David Fulton Publishers.

Middleton, T., ahmed Shafi, A., Millican, R. and Templeton, S. (2020) 'Developing effective assessment feedback: academic buoyancy and the relational dimensions of feedback', *Teaching in Higher Education: Critical Perspectives.* DOI: 10.1080/13562517.2020.1777397

Punch, K. (2009) *Introduction to Research Methods in Education.* London: Sage.

Punch, K. and Oancea, A. (2014) *Introduction to Research Methods in Education.* 2nd edn. London: Sage.

Roberts-Holmes, G. (2018) *Doing Your Early Years Research Project: A Step-by-Step Guide.* 4th edn. London: Sage.

Rose, J. (2006) *Independent Review of the Teaching of Early Reading, Final Report*, March 2006. Nottingham: DfES Publications.

Sagor, R. (2011) *The Action Research Guide Book: A Four-stage Process for Educators and School Teams.* 2nd edn. Thousand Oaks, CA: Corwin.

Sagor, R.D. and Williams, C. (2017) *The Action Research Guidebook: A Process for Pursuing Equity and Excellence in Education.* 3rd edn. Thousand Oaks, CA: Corwin.

Sharp, J. (2012) *Success with Your Education Research Project.* 2nd edn. London: Learning Matters.

Silverman, D. (2017) *Doing Qualitative Research.* 5th edn. London: Sage.

Taber, K. (2013) *Classroom-based Research and Evidence-based Practice.* 2nd edn. London: Sage.

Thomas, G. (2017) *How to Do Your Research Project: A Guide for Students.* 3rd edn. London: Sage.

Walliman, N. and Buckler, S. (2016) *Your Dissertation in Education.* 2nd edn. London: Sage.

Wilson, E. (2017) 'Data collection', in E. Wilson (ed.), *School-based Research: A Guide for Education Students.* 3rd edn. London: Sage, pp. 175–201.

Wragg, E. (2012) *An Introduction to Classroom Observation.* Classic edn. Abingdon: Routledge.

Wragg, E. and Brown, G. (2001) *Questioning in the Primary School.* Abingdon: Routledge.

Wyse, D. (2012) *The Good Writing Guide for Education Students.* 3rd edn. London: Sage.

WEBSITES

British Educational Research Association (BERA) Available at: www.bera.ac.uk

Education Endowment Fund (EEF) Available at: www.educationendowmentfoundation. org.uk

INDEX